101 Things to Do on the Street

by the same author

Working with Young Women
Activities for Exploring Personal, Social and Emotional Issues
2nd edition
ISBN 978 1 84905 095 1

Working with Young Men
Activities for Exploring Personal, Social and Emotional Issues
2nd edition
ISBN 978 1 84905 101 9

Let's Talk Relationships
Activities for Exploring Love, Sex, Friendship
and Family with Young People
2nd edition
ISBN 978 1 84905 136 1

Cyberbullying
Activities to Help Children and Teens to Stay Safe in a
Texting, Twittering, Social Networking World
ISBN 978 1 84905 105 7

of related interest

Helping Adolescents and Adults to Build Self-Esteem
A Photocopiable Resource Book
Deborah M. Plummer
ISBN 978 1 84310 185 7

Street Wise
A Programme for Educating Young People about
Citizenship, Rights, Responsibilities and the Law
Sam Frankel
Foreword by Bishop Tim Stevens
ISBN 978 1 84310 680 7

Are You Okay?
A Practical Guide to Helping Young Victims of Crime
Pete Wallis
ISBN 978 1 84905 098 2

What Have I Done?
A Victim Empathy Programme for Young People
Pete Wallis with Clair Aldington and Marian Liebmann
ISBN 978 1 84310 979 2

101 Things to Do on the Street

Second Edition

Games and Resources for Detached, Outreach and Street-Based Youth Work

Vanessa Rogers

Jessica Kingsley *Publishers*
London and Philadelphia

First published in 2000 by the National Youth Agency as *Have You Ever? A Handbook of Resource Activities for Detached Youth Workers*

Second edition published in 2011
by Jessica Kingsley Publishers
116 Pentonville Road
London N1 9JB, UK
and
400 Market Street, Suite 400
Philadelphia, PA 19106, USA

www.jkp.com

Library of Congress Cataloging in Publication Data
Rogers, Vanessa.
  101 things to do on the street : games and resources for detached, outreach and street-based youth work / Vanessa Rogers. -- 2nd ed.
      p. cm.
  "First published in 2000 by the National Youth Agency as Have You Ever-- ? A Handbook of Resource Activities for Detached Youth Workers."
  ISBN 978-1-84905-187-3 (alk. paper)
 1. Social work with youth. 2. Recreational therapy for youth. 3. Games--Social aspects. 4. Youth workers. I. Rogers, Vanessa. Have you ever--? II. Title. III. Title: One hundred one things to do on the street. IV. Title: One hundred and one things to do on the street.
  HV1421.R64 2011
  362.7--dc22
                              2010030856

British Library Cataloguing in Publication Data
A CIP catalogue record for this book is available from the British Library

ISBN 978 1 84905 187 3

Printed in Great Britain by the MPG Books Group

Contents

Acknowledgements

I would like to thank Ingrid Davies (Youth Offending Team), Richard Jenkins (Leggatts Youth Centre), Gareth Wynne (Youth Programmes – Education Welfare Services (EWS)), Nick Hayfield (Potters Bar Detached Team), Ann McKay (Hertfordshire County Council (HCC) Youth Service), Lorraine Clark (Young Citizen's Project), Richard Wood, Mike Smith (Community Development Team), John Weinstock (Outdoor Education Team), Charlotte Rogers, Ian Marchant (Pioneer Youth Centre), David Moses, Mary Westgate (HCC Youth Service), Tony Hunt (HCC Learning Services), North London Line, Chrysalis Drugs Project, Jani Noakes (EWS), Gillian Porter, Hazel Ashley, Fiona Factor and Deborah Mulroney.

Thanks also to any other youth workers not mentioned who have been part of the detached projects referred to in this book.

About the Author

Vanessa Rogers is a qualified teacher and youth worker with a Master's degree in community education. She has over ten years' experience within the Hertfordshire Youth Service both at practitioner and management levels. Prior to achieving national recognition for her work, Vanessa managed a wide range of services for young people including a large youth centre and targeted detached projects for Hertfordshire County Council. She devises and delivers professional development training programmes and writes for *Youth Work Now*. In addition she has been commissioned to devise training packs for a wide range of organisations, including the BBC.

This book is one of 20 resources written by Vanessa to support the development of creative youth work and social education.

Her website, www.vanessarogers.co.uk, gives detailed information about further titles, training and consultancy visits.

Introduction

Detached work is nothing new. It makes a valuable contribution to the rich and chequered history of youth work, remaining popular worldwide for the simple reason that it works: engaging young people who do not access centre-based youth services in positive activities that they enjoy and see value in.

As a new detached worker, I hit the streets armed with enthusiasm and a whole load of knowledge about the theory of detached work. I pretty soon realised that, valuable as this was, I didn't have much idea of what to do with young people once I had made contact. Although it was great to chat and build relationships, it became ever more important to think of ways to take the work to the next level, so that the young people could actually participate in something that they were developing, exploring issues important to them and potentially gaining a positive voice in their community.

This book contains a collection of ideas for games, projects and activities that explore a wide range of issues, including teambuilding, citizenship, positive relationships and bullying, that started life as a bundle of ideas that were used on the streets time and time again. Over the years these have been added to by my detached team and other street-based workers, resulting in 101 ideas that have been tried and tested in the field.

I do not claim the collection to be definitive! I am sure there are loads more brilliant activities that have not been included – if yours is one of them, please let me know!

Detached, outreach or mobile?

The main difference between detached youth work and centre-based work is that detached youth workers enter the 'space' occupied by young people. However, over the long history of street-based youth work, there has been much debate over the difference between detached, outreach and mobile youth work. Although the idea of working with young people where they meet, be it on the street, in a park or shopping mall, remains the same, for me there are clear differences between each approach.

In short, detached youth work involves engaging young people where they are and developing projects that take place in that environment. Successful detached projects have always been dependent on youth workers' remarkable skills to develop positive relationships. With no high-tech gadgets or warm buildings to entice young people in, street-based work is highly dependent on the detached workers' communication skills and ability to undertake a comprehensive needs analysis, enabling them to develop quality projects in response. This approach offers young people the opportunity to explore issues, discover and develop interests and build skills for the future.

Outreach work differs in that the over-arching aim is to get to know young people and then encourage them to use other specific provision (e.g. youth clubs, sexual health or counselling services), usually building based. Finally, mobiles provide a mobile youth club on the street, great for rural areas or districts that have few youth facilities. The van or bus becomes the youth centre and work takes place from there. Some mobiles bring specific services such as health, mini-cinema or art projects to an area, while others offer a generic youth club.

All three youth work interventions have their own unique strengths and provide a forum for good youth work to take place.

Why choose 'detached youth work'?

Good detached work doesn't happen in isolation: it should be a part of the overall youth services for an area. There should be clear reasons for choosing detached work as the most effective vehicle for delivering quality youth work in an area that can demonstrate how it meets the needs of a particular group of young people, rather than seeing it as an easy, quick 'fix all' solution or cheap option.

As with any youth work, the role of a detached youth worker is to support young people through a curriculum that has clear aims and objectives. This can include offering them the opportunity to work towards some form of accreditation. This autonomy and freedom from a building gives a detached youth worker a high level of flexibility in order to meet the changing needs of young people. It also takes time and commitment, on the part of both the detached team and the young people.

Working in partnership on the street

Increasingly, street-based workers are working in partnership with other agencies to deliver projects. While this has distinct benefits (e.g. it can be more cost effective and open up access to specialist services), it also presents a whole series of issues. As a guide, make sure that before any work actually takes place the following have been considered and agreed.

What are the aims of the detached project?

Detached work is about developing and delivering work in the place where young people choose to meet. Law enforcement agencies, such as the police, may have a different agenda – for example, 'getting kids off the streets'. This conflict of interests is best discovered before you have engaged with the young people.

Which young people are you going to work with?

Street-based work is a voluntary engagement between youth workers and young people. Some partners may think that, because an area or a group of young people has been identified as appropriate for intervention, the youths have to comply. This is not so: not all young people are delighted by the fact that workers are coming into their territory, and young people will vote with their feet if they see no value in what is on offer.

Who else may be working in the area with young people?

It is really important, before planning a detached project, that some research is done to find out who else might already be working on the streets. From statutory agencies, such as the police or youth offending services, through to community cohesion workers and church groups, there are some excellent examples of youth work skills being used by other agencies to engage teenagers on the streets. There is no point in duplicating work if there is already a successful project in place; instead, consider if there is scope for adding value to it by offering your agency in partnership.

Who are potential partners?

Arguably, street-based work has been adopted by a wider range of agencies and community groups now than at any time in its history, providing a wealth of potential partners. This is particularly true of targeted detached projects, where a group of young people is identified as being either 'at risk' of anti-social and/ or offending behaviour or vulnerable. Faith-based groups often use a detached approach; other potential partners include drug and alcohol agencies, sexual health teams and, more recently, police community support officers and street wardens. Each potential partner offers scope for creative projects, but make sure the terms of the partnership are agreed in advance.

Who is the lead agency?

It could be the specialist agency commissioning the work (e.g. health services or the organisation funding it, such as a community safety partnership). It could mean those responsible for writing reports and deciding an exit strategy, especially if the project is funded by a charity or grant.

Who is funding the project?

Money and funding can lead to issues around power and responsibility. Make sure it is agreed who answers to funders and that your project can deliver their requirements. A classic example of this is funding given to move young people away from their current meeting point. Does this fit with the ethos of detached work? If not, is this going to be an outreach project and are all partners signed up to this? In this way, everyone is clear about the aims and objectives of the work, and understands that these are unlikely to include getting young people 'off the streets'.

What expectations do partners have of each other?

For example, a funder may expect work to be undertaken effectively and completed within 12 weeks, whereas an experienced detached worker might consider this time part of the trust- and relationship-building phase of a project and not expect any real interventions to take place for another 6 weeks or so.

Are there shared values between agencies?

Particularly around topics such as drugs and alcohol or sex and relationships, issues can arise between partners with no shared vision that make it difficult to move forward. The time to discover that your partner works to a totally different set of values from that of your own organisation is not in front of a group of young people you have spent weeks trying to engage. Before starting, discuss approaches to issues such as abortion, abstinence, delaying early pregnancy, sexual health and offending behaviour to make sure you can accommodate all partners' values.

Can anyone be a detached worker?

Well, in my opinion yes and no! While anyone can walk the streets saying 'Hello' to any person under 18, it takes a certain skills set and confidence to move this on and encourage young people to meet regularly and get involved in projects. However, these can be developed over time and with experience. The collection of resources in this book aims to support the process of developing quality detached youth work interventions that encourage young people to participate, learn and have fun!

Key factors for success

1. Planning

Detached youth work should be planned. Without it, after the initial stages of checking out the area, observing where young people hang out and then beginning to get to know them, it can quickly turn into a series of 'chats'. While this might be fun for everyone involved, it can have little or no impact on young people.

2. Scoping

It is important that detached work responds to need, rather than be delivered as a 'one size fits all' model. The ideas included in this book are intended as a starting point to enable workers to explore topics and create interest among young people. This can lead to wider projects that respond to need.

3. Delivering

Positive outcomes for young people take time to deliver and detached work is not a 'quick fix' solution. This needs to be conveyed to other agencies to avoid unrealistic expectations.

Good detached work develops out of regular contact with young people over time.

4. Evaluation

Reports and recordings should provide a thorough evaluation of work undertaken. They should be clear enough for people not involved in detached youth work to understand its effectiveness. If, over a period of time, a detached project is unable to demonstrate any real change or progress towards the targets set, then a decision needs to be made about the validity of continuing the work.

5. Exit strategy

Almost from the first contact, detached youth workers are working towards saying goodbye. It is important that young people know that the work is time bound, and that a good exit strategy is put in place to ensure that the project doesn't just wither and die, or leave young people feeling abandoned and let down. Be honest from the start and celebrate the end of the project with the young people so that there is a clear finish.

Staying safe on the street

One of the main issues for street projects is maintaining both youth workers' safety and that of the young people they are working with. It is important to remember that, if you are planning to work where young people choose to meet, you are going into their territory and there may be occasions when this is not welcome!

Before you start

Get to know your area thoroughly – for example, hospitals, police stations, late night take-away restaurants, etc. – and have a list of phone numbers for local agencies. Inform the local police and other organisations in the area about your project, and let them know when and where you are likely to be operating. Make contact with local residents, shopkeepers, churches and schools, and tell them about your project too.

One of the most important roles detached workers may have is to signpost and support young people to access specialist services, so find out what is available in the area. Working closely with young people and building trusting relationships takes time and it can be tempting to try and take on all areas of support in their lives. However, it is important to keep within professional boundaries and know when to refer or consider bringing in specialist workers.

In your organisation

Managers, colleagues and partnership agencies need to understand that the process required to work effectively with young people in a detached setting is different from mainstream provision. Detached youth workers can feel isolated from centre-based workers and need good team and management support to avoid this.

It is important for safe practice to set up appropriate support structures before any street project begins. Always make sure that someone knows where you are going and when and whom is to be called when the session ends or in an emergency. Consider agreeing a 'code word' or sentence that means you need assistance or help. In real emergencies, contact the police first.

On the streets

Be open with young people as to who you are, why you are there and how long you are planning to work with them. Set out clear boundaries about confidentiality and the scope of your work in order to dispel any unrealistic expectations. On the streets it can be easy for both young people and workers to forget these boundaries, so take opportunities regularly to reinforce the things you can and cannot keep confidential. Consider this safety checklist:

1. Always tell the organisation you work for where you are going and when.

2. Take a mobile with you and have an emergency contact number for out of hours.

3. Work in pairs and agree boundaries and practice before you go out.

4. Inform the local police who you are and where the street project is taking place.

5. Make sure your recordings are accurate and thorough.

6. Always approach young women from the front so that they can see you.

7. Never give out your home address or phone number – make sure young people are aware of your professional boundaries.

8. Carry ID badges in case members of the community challenge you or young people want confirmation of what you say.

9. Don't work with young people who have obviously been drinking alcohol or using drugs. Make an agreement to meet up another time.

10. Act within the law and if you feel unsafe or unsure at any time – leave immediately!

At the end of the session

Make sure your recordings are accurate and thorough. Employers are entitled to expect staff to comply with agency guidelines and policies, as well as to understand and act upon legal requirements, such as child protection procedures. While it may not be appropriate for workers to openly condemn inappropriate behaviour on the street, they don't have to condone it, and any concerns should be recorded and line managers informed.

Evaluate each session, preferably with the young people, to reflect on learning and aid the planning process. Finally, text or call your contact to tell them that you have finished work.

Basic kit bag

A basic kit bag is a really useful accessory for detached youth work. I am not suggesting that you pack up the entire contents of the local youth centre, but a selection of 'things' to do means that you never run out of ideas. An ideal bag is a sports holdall with lots of compartments to divide up into areas for information, health and safety, basic tools and equipment for activities and projects. The young people will start to feel a sense of ownership towards its contents and look forward to seeing what you have packed each week.

Depending on where you plan to work, we have often taken a blanket out in the summer to use as a base. This means that the young people can put their belongings down in a relatively safe place while they take part in whatever you have planned. It also encourages them to stay around longer because they can sit and chat with workers as well as each other. Finally, it makes it easier for you to be found next time.

The list shown is not a blueprint, but one that I have put together in consultation with different detached teams that each had things they would not be without.

Mobile phone ID card/badge Emergency phone numbers Personal alarm Bottle of water Small towel Torch (and batteries!)	Leaflets – local youth services – sexual health – drugs and alcohol Condoms (if appropriate) Tampons or sanitary towels
Ball Pack of cards Juggling balls Markers Flipchart paper Dice 'Yo-yo's	Whatever is needed for the week's session Consent forms Risk assessment – if needed

How to use this resource

This book has been divided into four sections – Icebreakers, Activities and Games, Projects and Evaluation. Each session has been specifically designed to build a curriculum over several weeks or alternatively to be used as a standalone activity. Simply choose the session that you want to facilitate and photocopy any worksheets and resources.

All the activities are ideal for street-based work for the following reasons.

1. They are specifically designed to be used on the streets or in an outdoor environment, including parks and on the beach.

2. They have been developed using a range of learning styles and many offer alternative delivery methods for young people with additional needs.

3. They need little or no equipment – essential if you have to carry it!

4. They are cheap and easy to prepare.

5. They work with small or larger groups of young people and can be adapted on the spot.

Who is this book for?

The resources offer creative ideas for anyone planning to engage young people aged 11–19 in social education outside building-based provision. Suitable for seasoned detached, outreach or mobile workers, they are also a useful compendium of ideas for novice street workers.

All the activities are shown as group work activities (for 6 to 12 young people) but they can be altered to facilitate larger numbers or scaled down for smaller groups. As young people come from a wide range of cultural, ethnic, faith and economic backgrounds, numerous individual factors have been considered and alternative delivery options have been suggested, where possible, to ensure that the pack is inclusive.

Some participants in the sessions may have very low self-esteem or counselling needs that cannot be met on the streets, so a strategy for support should be agreed beforehand and appropriate services identified. The issues explored also make the activities appropriate for those working with targeted youth aiming to reduce anti-social behaviour and offending.

Consent forms

If you plan to engage young people in activities that need a risk assessment, or that will move them away from the area that you normally meet them in, you should always try and obtain parental or carers' consent. If the young people are over 18, they can give this themselves; if not, we have devised an 'activity consent form'. This was put together for street work and makes sure that parents, carers and young people are aware of the work that you plan to do. It also means that, if there is an accident or problem, you have the information to hand to support the young people. It can be easily altered to suit most events and activities.

How to do it

Prepare the 'activity consent forms'. The emergency number given for contacting the group during the session can be your mobile and/or the youth office.

Hand out copies of the form a week before you plan to start the project or activity. Examples of the need for consent forms are sessions like 'Bike circuits', 'Street barbecue', or 'Youth forum'.

Explain to the young people that you need them to show the forms to whomever has responsibility for their care, to get them signed and to return them before the session starts the next week.

Either you or your co-worker should assume responsibility for keeping the 'activity consent forms' for the duration of the session. If you are planning a series of sessions, put all the dates and details on the form, so it only has to go home once for signing.

After the project, the forms can be filed with your evaluation sheets.

ACTIVITY CONSENT FORM

Project or activity. . . . .

Place being visited (if appropriate). . . . .

Date . . . . / . . . . / . . .   From . . . .   Until . . . . . .   Meeting at . . . .

I give consent for . . . . (name of young person) to be allowed to take part in this event or trip and to participate in the activities involved.

Medical conditions

It is really important that we should know of any pre-existing medical condition (e.g. asthma, diabetes, heart trouble), which may require treatment and/or any condition that may affect participation in any activity.

Does the young person suffer from any pre-existing medical condition requiring treatment? Yes/No

If yes, ... (first name) suffers from . . . . which may require treatment.

Please list known allergies to drugs or other medication (e.g. antibiotics and plasters)

. . . .

Date of last immunisation against tetanus (if known) . . . . / . . . . / . . . .

NHS medical card number (if known) . . . .

Is there any other information that you think we should have? . . . .

. . . .

. . . .

I consent to any emergency medical treatment, including the use of anaesthetics, necessary during the course of the event.

Signature . . . . (Parent or Carer)   Date . . . . / . . . . / . . . .

Address . . . .

. . . .

Telephone number . . . .

In case of emergency while the event is taking place please call . . . .

(full name) on . . . . For further information please contact the

Youth Office on . . . .

Ground rules

It is a really good idea to agree 'ground rules' or a 'contract' with young people early on in the detached project. It provides boundaries, but also gives the opportunity for the whole group to participate in an activity that has a clear outcome. These can be revisited as new members join the project and old ones move on, and they provide a focus for any issues that arise within the sessions.

Make sure that you are clear and straight with the young people from the first meeting about where your confidentiality ends. Ensure that both you and they are aware of the boundaries set for the group, and your legal duty regarding child protection issues. That way everyone knows that you may have a duty to act upon information they give, and that they have a choice about how much they share.

How to do it

Ask the young people what 'rules' would make their sessions with you work better, and encourage them to respect difference within the group. Explain that these are not rules you are imposing, but group boundaries, which will include youth workers. All members of the group should participate and each point be agreed by all before it goes on the list.

Write ideas up on a flipchart sheet, which can then be signed by all taking part, dated and kept by the youth workers. Point out that, while you cannot enforce the rules in the same way that building-based workers might, you are asking people to sign up to them so there is time to discuss any issues raised. If there are any rules that, if broken, are likely to lead to the project ending or youth workers withdrawing, this is the time to point them out. These might include violent or aggressive behaviour to staff or openly engaging in criminal activities – for example, smoking cannabis.

None of the rules are set in stone and can be revisited as appropriate, especially as people join or leave the group.

Ground rules may include the agreement of all to:

- meet at a particular time

- not behave in a racist, sexist or any other discriminatory way

- do what was decided at the last session

- listen to other people without interrupting

- give respect to what people are saying

- be open to new ideas

- recognise that we are all different and not to judge others.

Chapter 1

Icebreakers

1.1 Fruit salad

This icebreaker works best with groups of eight and more, with both young people and youth workers taking part. If you have a smaller group, use less fruit! It is fast and fun, and good with groups that you have not worked with before.

Aim

To open up dialogue between young people and youth workers.

You will need

- stones.

How to do it

Ask the young people to each find a stone and stand in a circle. They should then place their stone in front of them to mark a 'home' place. A youth worker stands in the middle of the circle and, going around the group, names the participants 'apples, oranges, lemons or pears…' This includes the youth workers!

The youth worker in the middle then calls out the fruit that they have been named – for example, apples. All 'apples' then swap places, including the youth worker. The person left without a home stone goes into the middle, calls another fruit and attempts to regain a home stone. At any time the person in the middle can call 'Fruit salad!' and everyone has to move.

Make sure that the group is well spaced out or it will become difficult to see who is 'home' and who is next in the middle.

1.2 Match it!

This is really a different version of 'Fruit salad' and works well with older young people. Be aware that it can get personal! You can use it as an introduction to a specific issue-based session.

Aim

To highlight commonalities among the group and the youth workers.

You will need

- chalk.

How you do it

With one youth worker in the middle, ask the group to form a wide circle and each member to mark their space with a chalk cross. This then becomes a 'safe' spot.

The person in the middle then calls out 'Everybody with…' This has to be something true for them as well as potentially true for other members of the group. Everyone that this includes then runs around the outside of the circle as fast as they can to a safe spot. The person who does not get a safe spot then goes into the middle and the process starts again.

Ideas

- Everyone who has blue eyes.
- Everyone who has a tattoo.
- Everyone who likes chocolate.
- Everyone who watches MTV.
- Everyone who plays football.
- Everyone who is vegetarian.

Make sure that everyone in the group is included and that participants don't manipulate the game to isolate others. Also don't call out things you are not prepared to explain – for example, where your tattoo is!

1.3 Marshmallow towers

Aim

To build the highest tower using marshmallows and spaghetti!

You will need

- packs of spaghetti
- marshmallows
- a watch.

How to do it

Divide the young people into teams of no more than six. Explain that the task is to design and construct the highest and most ornate tower without it collapsing. Explain that there is one rule: each team has to use the building materials given to them – then hand out the marshmallows and spaghetti!!

Encourage the young people to spend time planning and designing their tower first. If you want to offer a handy tip, the best way to construct it is to use the marshmallows to link the spaghetti together and build the tower up slowly in layers.

Allow 15 minutes to build the towers and then invite the groups to review each construction, commenting on design, height and teamwork. Award points for each and then decide the overall winner by counting them up.

The teams can now eat their marshmallows!

1.4 Storm

If you want to facilitate this group warm-up, you will need to have a large number of young people taking part to create a really effective 'storm'. This is a great invitation for them to be as loud as they can!

Aim

To produce the sounds of a storm. It is a good introduction to group work because it will only happen if they work together to create the effect.

You will need

- nothing!

How to do it

Invite the young people to form a circle large enough that everyone can see each other.

Explain that together you are going to create a 'storm' with sound.

Then begin by slowly rubbing both hands together, and motion for the rest of the group to join in.

Once the whole group is rubbing hands, begin to click your fingers, encouraging the others to follow. By this point the young people will have got the idea that they should follow whatever action you do.

As the noise of the finger clicking rises, change the clicking to clapping. Encourage the group to be as loud as possible!

Finally, bring the noise up to a crescendo by stamping feet while continuing clapping. Allow the full effect of the storm to be felt for a minute or so.

As the 'storm' rages, slowly stop stamping your feet. As the young people follow, begin to gradually halt the movements in reverse, allowing space for each stage.

Bring the noise back down to hand rubbing only and then slowly end.

1.5 Animals at the water hole

This is a good opportunity to explore how the young people you plan to work with see themselves. The fantasy element of the activity allows the group members to be open without exposing too much of themselves.

Aim

To begin to look at how the group members see themselves, and discuss if this differs from their public personae.

You will need

- Post-it® notes
- pens
- a large sheet of paper with a blue pond or 'water hole' drawn on it.

How to do it

Place the sheet of paper with the pond drawn on it into the middle of the group. Explain to the young people that this is a water hole. Go on to embellish your description by telling the group that this is the only water hole for miles, and that all the animals locally come here. Depending on your group, you can be as creative as you like to build this part up.

Hand out a Post-it note and pen to each group member. Ask them all to think about which animals they would choose to represent themselves at the water hole, and then write the names of the animals on their Post-it notes. Inform the young people that you are not asking them to put their own names on their notes, but that you will be inviting them to talk about what they chose later.

Finally ask them to stick their Post-it notes by the water hole where they think they should be.

When everybody has placed their 'animal' by the water hole, gather the group together to see what is there. Facilitate a discussion around what animals have been chosen. Which animal has been chosen most? Why? Invite individuals to share what they have chosen and the reasons why. For example, 'My name is Raj and I chose an eagle so that I can fly away and be free when I want.' Is this a surprise? How does this fit with how others see Raj in the group? Does it fit with the image he projects?

1.6 Paper towers

This initial teambuilding activity is used to encourage young people to plan and work together. Any size group can take part and it works well for most age groups.

Aim

To encourage young people to work in groups to achieve a shared goal.

You will need

- newspaper
- sticky tape
- a watch.

How to do it

Divide the young people into groups, no more than six in each group. Explain that you want them to plan and then construct paper towers. The object is to build the highest tower without it collapsing. Hand out newspaper and sticky tape.

During the planning, each member of the group should contribute and no building can take place without the whole group's approval.

Give the groups 15 minutes to build their towers – and stand well back!

1.7 Sign in

This is a good icebreaker to use with young people whom you think will not want to engage in anything that they consider is too much like 'games'.

Aim

To find out the names of the young people you plan to work with and give them yours.

You will need

- flipchart paper
- selection of marker pens.

How to do it

Ask each of the young people to 'sign in' to the group. They can give their full names or street names – whatever they want to be known as.

Make sure that the youth workers do the same.

Ask about any unusual designs or names, and open up discussions.

If you want to take this further, encourage the group members to put faces after their names that show how they feel – for example, a smiley face! Depending on how creative the group is, you could develop this further. If not, you now have the names of the entire group and they know yours.

Bring the sheet with you the following week so that newcomers can add their names to it.

1.8 My first CD warm-up

Aim

To create a fun opportunity for the group to get to know each other, and to open up discussions about musical preferences.

You will need

- Post-it notes
- pens
- a bowl.

How to do it

Hand each young person a pen and a Post-it note. They should all write down the name of the first CD they ever bought with their own money. Once they have done this, they should fold the paper into four, so that no one else can see it. When everyone has finished, collect the folded papers in the bowl.

Shake the bowl to mix up the papers and randomly pull one out, open it and read it aloud. The young person who guesses correctly whom it belongs to then selects the next paper to be opened.

Leave space between rounds to ask about choices and how musical tastes have or have not changed. Comment on the range of musical genres appreciated within the group.

1.9 Animal warm-up

Aim

To discover personality similarities and encourage discussion.

You will need

- five sheets of flipchart paper
- Blu-Tack®
- marker pens.

How to do it

Before the session, write the headings 'RABBIT', 'BEAR', 'HORSE', 'KANGAROO' and 'LION' onto flipchart sheets and stick them at different points on the pavement.

When the young people arrive, ask them to go and stand by the animal that they think most resembles their personality. Those by each animal should then discuss with each other why they selected that particular animal. For example, do the 'kangaroos' tend to jump around from thing to thing, full of energy? Are 'rabbits' quick and enthusiastic, or 'horses' hardworking and loyal or wild and fast?

Each group can then write up its shared characteristics onto the flipchart sheet under the heading.

Invite each animal group to share its characteristics with the rest of the groups.

1.10 Positive pictures

The ability to be assertive, rather than aggressive or passive, comes from understanding that, as a person, you have value.

Aim

To encourage participants to explore both their personal and others' view of their behaviour.

You will need

- A4 paper (approx. 8.5 x 11")
- Blu-Tack
- pens.

How to do it

Begin by handing the people in your group a piece of paper and telling them to use the paper to draw a picture of themselves. Remind reluctant participants that this is not an art contest.

Once the self-portraits are complete, ask each person to turn the paper over and write five words they would use to accurately describe themselves. Encourage them to use the first five words that come to mind. Once the participants have finished this task, place them in pairs or small groups and ask them to show their drawings to each other.

Ask them to pay particular attention to things like how much space the drawing takes up or whether positive or negative words were used in the description. Once they have had a chance to look at other people's drawings, ask everyone to analyse their own work and share any insights with the group. Then ask group members to stick their pictures on the wall and ask everyone to spend a moment writing something positive on each picture. Conclude the exercise by redistributing the pictures and allowing members to read the positive statements other people have written about them.

1.11 Be your own hero

Aim

To enable young people to identify the traits and skills that they admire in others, and to look at ways to develop their own.

You will need

- nothing!

How to do it

Ask the young people the question 'Who is your hero?' Explain that, if they don't have one, they can try to think of someone who has characteristics that they admire or wish they had. Make sure that you stress that these heroes may be real, fictional, dead or alive. Ask the group to discuss what it is about the person they have chosen that they admire.

Next, ask the young people to think of a scenario from the past that did not go as well as they would have liked. This can be a problem experienced at home, school or college, an interaction with another person, a job they didn't get – anything. Ask them to explain the scenario as they remember it happening, including the negative outcome. You may want to revisit the ground rules here.

Now, in groups, ask the young people to re-enact or discuss the situation but this time in the character of their hero. Was the outcome positive this time? What was it that made it different? To end, review and ask what it was that made their hero able to cope, and whether any of these skills are transferable to their own lives – for example, being assertive, being able to say what they wanted, etc. Share one point in a circle and close the session.

1.12 Group shapes

This is a simple game but needs co-operation and should be played at a fast pace. It is a good warm-up to use as part of a team-building session.

Aim

To encourage the group to work together.

You will need

- a large clear space.

How to do it

Ask the young people to walk around the room, using all the space and trying not to bump into each other. Then call out a shape, which the whole group must form. This shape must include everyone – start with a circle because this is easy!

Between making shapes, ask the young people to walk around steadily as before, using all the space in the room. You can speed up how rapidly you ask them to form shapes as they get the hang of the game! Other shapes that work well are:

- a triangle
- a square

- a diamond

- any capital letter

- a star (five points).

Once the game is over, review the process. Did any leaders emerge? How easy was it to include everyone?

1.13 Values and attitudes activity

During this activity, young people get to share and discuss their values and attitudes around a whole range of issues. The duration of the exercise is flexible, depending on the young people concerned and their willingness to share personal feelings. You can adapt the 'tree key' to meet the needs of the group.

Aim

To explore similarities and differences within the group.

You will need

- flipchart paper

- coloured marker pens.

How to do it

Divide the young people into groups of 3–5 with marker pens and a sheet of flipchart paper per team.

Each group's task is to draw a tree on the sheet. The tree must include roots, a trunk, branches, leaves, buds, fruit, flowers and thorns.

Tree Key

Roots = life influences and beliefs

Trunk = life structure, and particularly aspects that are firm and fixed

Branches = relationships and interests

Leaves = skills

Buds = ideas and hopes for the future

Fruit = achievements

Flowers = individuality and strengths

Thorns = challenges, threats and difficulties

Ask each team to share and discuss their trees and interpretations with the rest of the group. Emphasise the need for active listening and non-judgemental feedback, and encourage discussion about similarities and differences.

1.14 Spin the bottle

This is a fast activity that can be used almost anywhere. If the group is large, stick with names; if it is small, improvise and add detail!

Aim

To enable the group and the youth workers to become familiar with everyone's name.

You will need

- a plastic bottle – check to see that it spins well before you go out!

How to do it

Stand or sit in a circle – including the youth workers. Ask for a volunteer to start the activity. Ask the person to spin the bottle and say, 'I'm…' The person whom the bottleneck faces when it stops spinning takes the bottle, spins it again, says 'I'm…' and then gives the name of the person who spun it last. This continues with all participants adding their names to the list as they spin the bottle.

Make sure that you are somewhere towards the end of this process if possible. If you cannot do this, make it clear that it is OK if someone forgets a name – just ask the person to repeat it and continue. Similarly, be aware that those who went first do not put pressure on those with a harder task!

1.15 Hello I'm…

This works best with large groups that do not know each other well. We have used it to bring two groups together for a summer project.

Aim

To get to know names and encourage the young people to work together to complete the task.

You will need

- nothing!

How to do it

Sit in a large circle or in a line. The first person says 'Hello I'm…' and turns to the next person. That person in turn says, 'Hello I'm…', turns back to the last person and continues, 'This is…'

The process continues, becoming more difficult as the number of names increases! Make sure that the youth workers are placed in the middle and at the end so that they can support anyone who is struggling. However, in my experience this is often the youth workers because all the names are new to them!

1.16 Reflective listening

Aim

To introduce the concept of reflective listening to the group. It encourages the young people to listen carefully to what is being said and to reflect on it, rather than cutting in with their own opinions.

You will need

- nothing!

How to do it

Depending on the number of young people you have in the group, ask them to work in threes or fours. If it is a really small group, it does work in pairs. Discuss confidentiality at this stage and reach an agreement that what is shared in the group stays within the group. This should encourage the participants to feel safe about talking personally.

Specify a topic to discuss within the group – for example, 'What people usually think about me when they first meet me is…' You can demonstrate this by giving an example to start them off: 'What people usually think about me when they first meet me is that I have a good sense of humour!' If you think that the group might be nervous, choose something less personal like 'One thing I really hate/like is…'

Set a ground rule that only one member can talk at a time in the group, and that the others should listen and think about what is being said.

Once each person has had a say, discuss the following within the groups.

1. How similar was what your friend said to what you actually thought when you first met each other?

2. Does your self-image correspond to what others think of you?

3. Are there similar themes and issues?

1.17 Pairs

I think that this probably works best with groups of young people who do not know each other well.

Aim

To encourage the young people to talk to each other and the youth workers and open up a dialogue.

You will need

* a set of the 'pairs cards'

* a few spare cards in case you have too many young people and have to improvise.

How to do it

Hand out a card to each young person. If you have an odd number of people, take a card yourself. Invite the group to look at their cards, but not to tell anybody else what is written on them. It does not matter if you have duplicate 'pairs', so long as each person can find a partner.

Ask the young people to go off and 'find' their pair. They can only do this by asking indirect questions – for example, they cannot ask, 'Are you a nurse?' but they could ask, 'Do you work in a hospital?' When they find each other, they should tell each other their names and remain together until the large group reforms.

PAIRS CARDS

Musician	Fan	Artist	Model
Nurse	Patient	Teacher	Pupil
Parent	Child	Police officer	Criminal
Actor	Audience	Sales assistant	Customer
Footballer	Coach	Taxi driver	Passenger
Waiter	Diner	DJ	MC
Lecturer	Student		

1.18 Picture pairs

This is a version of 'Pairs' that can be used with young people who have difficulties in reading and prefer to work with pictures.

Aim

To get the young people and the youth workers talking to each other as they find their 'pair'.

You will need

- a set of 'pairs cards' – enough for each member of the group
- spare cards (in case you are surprised by numbers).

How to do it

Before you go out on the streets, make up a set of cards by sticking picture 'pairs' onto A6 (approx. 4 x 6") pieces of card or stiff paper. You can be as creative as you like with the pictures. They could be simple hand-drawn images or shapes. I have cut photos out of magazines that are of the same celebrity or article, and used them – for example, logos, pop stars and footballers. I have also used celebrity couples such as David and Victoria Beckham.

Hand out a picture card to each young person and worker. Ask everyone to look at their cards and then to put them away. Make sure that each person has a potential pair. If you have an odd number, one of the workers needs to 'sit out' and support anyone who needs it.

Ask the young people to go around the group and 'find' their pair. Explain that they can ask questions but not directly. Once they have found their partners, ask them to exchange names and stay together until everyone is in pairs.

1.19 Birthdays

You can do this with any age and ability, but you really need more than 12 in the group for it to work well.

Aim

To enable the young people to make contact with each other and discover commonalties between each other and the youth workers.

You will need

- nothing!

How to do it

Ask the young people to find someone born in the same month as them. If this is no challenge because they all know each other very well, choose another date that they are all likely to know – for example, a parent's birthday.

When they have found a partner, ask them to join with another pair born in the same month and repeat until the whole group is divided into months.

Once everyone is in a 'month' group, ask the young people to share the dates of their birthdays and arrange themselves in descending order.

Finally, facilitate the whole group to get into a circle or line that starts with January and goes through to December.

Review the process with the group.

1.20 I went to the shops

This is really just a memory game and can be used for as big a group as you like. The bigger the group the harder the game!

Aim

This game is a warm-up that brings the young people together with youth workers to produce a giant 'shopping list' that has to be memorised.

You will need

- nothing!

How to do it

Ask the group to form a large circle. Organise yourself and your co-worker at a distance to each other within the group.

You start by saying 'I went to the shops and I bought a loaf of bread.' The person to your left carries on with another item, adding it to yours – for example, 'I went to the shops and I bought a loaf of bread and an apple.'

This continues around the circle with each person adding something to the shopping list of things bought at the shop. As the game goes on the list gets longer!

If someone cannot remember or struggles, encourage the group to help. Make sure that a worker is always towards the end of the sequence and so has to take part in the 'difficult' bit!

Depending on the size of the group, this should take you about 15 minutes. For a variation you could set a theme, such as food, clothes or even cars.

1.21 Attitude scale

This icebreaker is a good way to start any work around assertiveness and self-image. Alternatively you can adapt it for use in other issue-based work by changing the subject of your scale.

Aim

To encourage the young people to think about how they see themselves, and to consider how this compares with how others perceive them.

You will need

- a watch.

How to do it

Explain to the young people that the aim of this activity is to develop an attitude scale, to show the personalities within the group ranging from 'assertive' to 'passive'. The scale should form a straight line and include everyone.

Decide which end of your scale is 'assertive' and which end is 'passive', and make sure that the young people are clear about this. Allow 5–10 minutes (depending on the size of the group) for the young people to decide where they think they should stand on the scale. Position yourself on the scale too.

When all the group members are comfortable with their positions on the scale, stop. Ask them to look around them and reflect on what they see. Are there any surprises? Does how they see themselves fit in with other people's perception of them? What about the youth workers? Discuss the positive and negative points of both ends of the scale.

1.22 Guess who?

Do not do this if you think individuals will feel uncomfortable. Depending on the ages of the young people and the size of the group, this can be a short exercise or take up to 30 minutes. The younger the group the quicker the game!

Aim

To discover things about each other and share information. This includes young people and youth workers so be prepared to share something!

You will need

- small squares of paper
- pens.

How to do it

Each person takes a piece of paper and writes on it something personal that the rest of the group does not know. You can make suggestions at this stage that make it clear that the idea is to be unusual or surprising, but not too private or intimate. For example, 'My dad used to be in a heavy metal band' is fine, but 'I saw Kelly's boyfriend with someone else' is not!

Ask the group to fold up their papers so no one can see what is on them and give them to a nominated person. Jumble up the papers and place them on the ground. Ask people in turn to step forward and pick up a paper. If they pick up their own, tell them to put it down under the others and take another.

The young people then move around and ask each other relevant questions to try and guess whose information they are holding. These questions must be indirect – for example, they could ask 'Is anyone in your family musical?' but not 'Is your dad the one who used to be in the band?'

When they are sure that they have 'guessed who', they can challenge their suspect! If the guess is correct, the rest of the group takes time out from questioning and listens as the information is shared.

When all the owners of the papers have been found, ask the group to review the process. Was it easy to guess? How? Reflect on the information shared, and the fact that there are things we do not know about people – assumptions should always be checked out.

1.23 You'd never guess!

This is a quick version of 'Guess who?' and works well with groups that know each other but do not know the youth workers.

Aim

To show that there are things that we do not know about people, even if we know them well. Encourage the young people to share information with each other and the youth workers.

You will need

- nothing!

How to do it

Ask the young people to form a circle. If you are working in a park or play area, encourage them to sit down.

Starting with one of the youth workers, invite the member of the group in turn to say their names and then share something about themselves that they think the rest of the group would not guess. For example, 'My name is Tara and I'm a youth worker on the estate. The thing I am sharing is that last weekend I sang karaoke!'

Make sure that you explain clearly that the idea is to share something that the rest of the group do not know and that may provoke further conversation, but it should not be something said only to shock or that will make someone else feel uncomfortable. It may also be good to agree that the information stays within the group.

At the end of the circle, review the information shared.

1.24 Number game

This is quick warm-up game, which can be used with larger groups and is suitable for most ages.

Aim

To enable all members of the group to get to know each other.

You will need

- nothing!

How to do it

Ask everyone in the group to form a large circle, and then stand within it. Give each of the group a number; you will be number one.

When everybody has a number, start by calling out two numbers between one and the highest number in the group – for example, 'Number 7 meet number 12.' These young people then go into the middle of the circle and introduce themselves by name to each other and to the rest of the group.

Encourage the group to keep the pace going so that there is no opportunity for anyone to be left out. This process continues until everyone has been in the middle at least once.

1.25 Juggling

This works best if at least one of the youth workers cannot juggle! The point is to engage with the young people and encourage them to join in as a group, not to show off your circus skills!

Aim

To encourage the young people to participate in an activity with the youth workers.

You will need

- at least six sets of soft juggling balls
- other juggling equipment if any of you can use it!

How to do it

Set up a base that you intend to work from for this session. In the summer we use a blanket if we are able to, because it encourages the young people to sit down and talk when they are not participating in the activity.

Begin to juggle; if one of you is not very good at it, let the more experienced juggler show you how. Make it clear that it does not matter if you cannot do it – the idea is to practise and have a go.

Once the group you are hoping to engage starts to show interest, invite the young people to come over and give them a set of balls. Usually this happens quickly, and in my experience there are always some members of the group who can juggle well. This can then become a two-way learning process as the young people show the youth workers and their peers how to juggle properly, and it is your opportunity to start learning about the group.

If they show an interest in juggling and want to develop further circus skills, consider taking out a diabolo, skittles or even a unicycle for future sessions.

1.26 Street questionnaire

This is really a game to introduce young people to each other and new youth workers. You could use it with established groups by altering the questions slightly to gain new information. I think that it works best with young people aged 12 or over. It is a good tool to use at the start of a project.

Aim

To find out information about each other within the group, and to discover differences, similarities and common interests.

You will need

- copies of the 'street questionnaire'
- plenty of pens.

How to do it

Ask one of the young people to hand out a questionnaire and pen to each member of the group.

Explain that what you want is a personal response – there are no right or wrong answers to the questions. You may want to point out that the information will be shared at the end with the group, so that the young people can choose what they wish to share.

Give the group about ten minutes to answer the questions, less if it is a really small group. They all then hand their sheets to the person on their left to read. This may be the time to remind the group members of any contract or agreement they have about respecting each other's views and confidentiality. Then, in turn, they all introduce the person whose questionnaire they hold.

You can end by facilitating a group discussion pulling out commonalities, similarities and differences within the group.

STREET QUESTIONNAIRE

1. What do you like to be called? . . . .

. . . .

2. How often do you come here?. . . . .

. . . .

3. If you could be anyone, whom would you be?. . . . .

. . . .

4. Why?. . . . .

. . . .

. . . .

. . . .

5. What is the most exciting thing you have ever done? . . . .

. . . .

. . . .

. . . .

. . . .

6. What is the most exciting thing you would like to do? . . . .

. . . .

. . . .

. . . .

. . . .

1.27 Run around

This should be fast and fun! It works with any age, but needs at least six young people to be effective.

Aim

To know each other's names by the end of the game.

You will need

- small slips of paper
- pens.

How to do it

Give all the young people a pen and a piece of paper to write their names on. Make sure you and your co-worker do it too!

Ask the group to make a circle with you in the middle.

If it is dry outside, place the pieces of paper in a pile on the floor beside you. If it is wet, put half in each pocket and draw them out from there!

Pick out two names, call them out and tell the young people to 'run around' to swap places. When you draw your own name, the other person whose name you call goes into the middle and so on.

Play until everybody has had the chance to 'run around'!

1.28 Beanbag game

This is a fast game, which can be a great way of encouraging a group to get to know each other. Make sure that the beanbag is being thrown *to* but not *at* anyone!

Aim

To share information within the group and to enable the young people and youth workers to get to know each others' names.

You will need

- a small, light beanbag.

How to do it

Gather the group together. You could form a circle but it is not essential. However, you do all need to be able to see each other.

All group members give their names and say something about themselves. I think the group responds well if a youth worker starts the process. For example, a worker could start by saying, 'I'm Sam and I like French fries!' or 'My name is Dylan and my dog is a great dane!' It is best to choose something that is memorable or funny, but not confrontational – for example, favourite sports teams.

Once everyone has spoken, the person holding the beanbag throws it to another group member and repeats what that person has said – for example, 'His name is Sam and he likes French fries!' The smaller the group, the further apart people need to stand to make this work effectively. Try and ensure that the beanbag is thrown to everyone and that the entire group has taken part.

The game ends when everybody has been introduced to each other.

1.29 Lemons

Aim

To introduce the idea of individual differences. It is a good exercise to use at the start of a session around equal opportunities.

You will need

- enough lemons for everyone in the group (or sweets, strawberries, nuts, etc.)
- a carrier bag.

How to do it

Give each group member a lemon.

Ask the young people to look closely at the fruit, examine it for distinctive marks and feel the skin. You can really act this part up if you want, using phrases like 'bonding' and 'getting in touch with'. Encourage the group members to personalise their lemons by naming them.

Give the group about 5 minutes to do this and then collect the lemons into the carrier bag.

Make a show of mixing the fruit up and shaking the bag. Then spread all the lemons out on the floor in front of the group.

Ask the young people to take it in turns to step forward and collect their lemons. If there is any argument, adjudicate, but, if they still can't agree, place the lemon to one side as 'unidentified'. If this happens, you should be left with two at the end to reunite. I have always been amazed that most young people can successfully claim their personal pieces of fruit.

Then facilitate a discussion. How sure are the young people that they claimed the correct fruit? How can they tell? Encourage them to look at the parallels between this exercise and differentiating between people. Look at stereotypes – are all lemons the same colour and shape? Reflect this into the stereotypes that exist between people of different cultures, races and gender. What does this mean to the group?

Your evaluation of this process will help you to develop further sessions around difference and equality of opportunity.

1.30 Shields

Shields can be used in small group situations with all ages. It is also a good way of encouraging young people with poor literacy skills to take part, because you can make it pictorial only.

Aim

To encourage young people to reflect on their lives so far, and to look at goals, wishes and feelings for the future.

You will need

- flipchart paper
- coloured marker pens.

How to do it

Give the young people sheets of paper and pens to work with. Take a sheet for yourself and draw a large shield shape in the middle. Ask everyone else to do the same. Explain that this is not a test of how well they can draw, and they do not have to have the same shaped shield.

Once everyone has a shield, ask everyone to divide each one into three equal areas. Once again, demonstrate this on yours. Explain that each third will represent a part of each person's life. One is the past and should show what has happened to date. The second is the present showing what is going on now, and the third is the future. The future can show all hopes, ambitions and dreams. Ask the young people where they see themselves in ten years' time. What will they be doing? Explain that the shield can include their hobbies, friends and families. The depth of the information on the shields will vary depending on how well you know the young people. When they have all completed their shields, bring the group back together and form a circle, inviting all to share the parts they feel comfortable sharing. Draw out similarities and discuss ideas. You can take this further at a later date to look at action plans for achievable goals.

1.31 If I could be…

This should be done quickly and works with any number of people. You can change your topic to suit the age and interests of the group.

Aim

This is an introduction game for everyone to share small pieces of personal information.

You will need

- nothing.

How to do it

Gather the group together and ask them to form a circle. This means that you can all see each other and should be able to hear what is said.

Explain to the group that, in order to begin to get to know them, you are going to ask them all to give their names. Then you would like them to think about whom they would choose to be if they could be a character in a TV show, and to give the reasons for their choice.

You can change the topic to anything that you think that the group will engage with. Suggestions include 'If I could be a:

- car, I would be a…because…
- colour, I would be…because…
- movie star, I would be…because…'

Ask the young person in turn to tell the group their name, and then introduce the character they have chosen, telling the group why they would like to be that person. It can be a good strategy to start the process off with your own ideas! Stop the game when everybody has had a turn and any comments or discussions that arise have been addressed.

Chapter 2

Activities and Games

2.1 Jobs for the boys?

This works well with mixed or same gender groups of up to ten. It should take about 15 minutes, but it can take longer with a larger group.

Aim

To explore gender stereotypes and provoke discussion.

You will need

- two A3 (approx. 11 x 17") size sheets of paper with 'AGREE' on one and 'DISAGREE' on the other
- Blu-Tack
- the 'statements' sheet.

How to do it

Ask the young people to listen to each statement and then move to either the 'AGREE' area or the 'DISAGREE' area. Stress that it is an individual response that you are looking for and that their first reaction is the one they should act on. If they are undecided, explain that they should stay put between the two areas. If they wish to change their opinion at any stage, they can, but encourage them to explain why.

After each movement, stop to discuss. If there is disagreement, ask the 'AGREE' group to explain to the 'DISAGREE' what they believe. Then ask the 'DISAGREE' group to respond.

If there is no disagreement invite the group to share their views and question them to provoke further thought.

STATEMENTS

1.	All male hairdressers are gay.
2.	Boys are better at science.
3.	Good mothers stay at home with their children.
4.	Men are better drivers than women.
5.	Girls go into jobs like teaching because females are naturally more caring.
6.	Young women shouldn't be able to compete in professional boxing.
7.	Nursing isn't a 'real' man's job.
8.	Fathers are able to care for their children just as well as mothers.
9.	Female football or soccer teams should be given the same TV coverage as male.
10.	Women make better secretaries because they are more organised than men.
11.	There are more men in management because they aren't as emotional as women.
12.	Car mechanics should be male because they understand engines better.
13.	Men should get the same leave as women when their babies are born.
14.	Women shouldn't be in the army.

2.2 Images

Aim

To raise the group's awareness of gender stereotyping in a non-confrontational way, encouraging them to open up further discussions.

You will need

- copies of the 'image cards' sheet (choose which to use)
- large sheets of paper
- marker pens.

How to do it

Hand each young person a slip from the 'image cards' sheet and a piece of paper. Explain that each slip has on it a job or description of what a person does.

Ask the participants to look at the word on their slip and then to draw a picture at the top of their paper of how they think that person looks. Stress that they should not tell anybody else what is on the slip at this stage. Allow a few minutes and then ask them to fold over that picture and pass their slip to the person nearest them. Repeat until all the slips have been circulated and then invite the young people to unfold their sheets of paper and show all their pictures.

Review what has been drawn. Are all the nurses shown as women? Are all the judges drawn as men? How about police and teachers? Encourage the group members to discuss how they decided what gender to draw. Look at stereotypes and if the pictures are actually representative of the profession shown.

IMAGE CARDS

Police officer	Lawyer
Sports coach	Head teacher
Nurse	Doctor
Chef	Social worker
Builder	Electrician
Model	Hairdresser
Cleaner	Truck driver
Judge	Car mechanic
Pilot	Secretary
Carpenter	DJ

2.3 Salt, pepper and vinegar

This is a fun activity that should not be taken too seriously! It works with the notion that most people want to belong to a group and, once an idea has been suggested that appeals to our self-image, we are more than happy to supply the rest!!

Aim

To explore self-image and belonging to a group.

You will need

- copies of the 'salt, pepper and vinegar characteristics' sheets
- three A4 sheets headed 'SALT', 'PEPPER' and 'VINEGAR'
- Blu-Tack.

How to do it

Before the young people arrive at the meeting place, stick the three named sheets in different places. The size of the space needed will depend on how many you are planning to work with.

Explain to the group members that the point of this exercise is to find similarities between them and to have fun, rather than any psychological insight the activity may give them. Stress it has no scientific basis whatsoever. Then read out the characteristic sheets for salt, pepper and vinegar. Because these are made up for the exercise, you can change them to make it more relevant to the group.

Ask the young people to listen carefully and think about which sheet they think sounds most like themselves. When they have decided whether they are salt, pepper or vinegar, ask them to go and gather by the appropriately labelled sheet of paper. Hand a copy of the characteristic sheet to each of the small groups.

Ask the young people to look again at the trademarks of each group, discuss how they think these apply to them, and agree similarities and differences. Then ask them, as a group, to identify five positive things about themselves and five areas of their collective group 'personality' that they would like to change.

Facilitate a group discussion.

1. How did people choose which group to join?

2. Could they identify with the other members of the group and the descriptions given?

3. Did it feel good to be part of the group?

4. What other groups do young people belong to? Why? What does being in a group offer?

SALT CHARACTERISTICS

Salts like:	Salt star signs:
Roast dinners	Libra
Disneyland	Cancer
Football	Sagittarius
Snow	Gemini
Family get-togethers	
Cuddly toys	
Barbecues	
Watching movies	
Key personality traits of Salts:	**Salt professions:**
Sharp	Fashion designer
Sporty	Professional boxer
Romantic	Carpenter
Traditional	Vet
Loving	Nanny
	Movie director
	Computer analysts
	Teacher
	Librarian

PEPPER CHARACTERISTICS

Peppers like:	Pepper star signs:
Curry	Leo
Gold jewellery	Aries
Theme parks	Capricorn
Cartoons	Taurus
Dancing	
Lying in the sun	
Working out at the gym	
Travelling	

Key personality traits of Peppers:	Pepper professions:
Generous	Model
Full of life	Hairdresser
Sensuous	Graphic designer
Outrageous	Youth worker
Funny	Beautician
	Photographer
	Landscape gardener
	Chef
	Builder

VINEGAR CHARACTERISTICS

Vinegars like:	**Vinegar star signs:**
Pizza	Aquarius
The zoo	Virgo
Online gaming	Pisces
Clubbing	Scorpio
Springtime	
Skateboarding	
Silver jewellery	
The beach	
Key personality traits of Vinegars:	**Vinegar professions:**
Sentimental	Interior designer
Mysterious	Motorbike stunt artist
Dramatic	Police officer
Passionate	DJ
Loyal	Sports referee
	Judge
	Singer
	Social worker
	Artist

2.4 Act out!

This activity can be used as a 'taster' for more in-depth drama or role-play sessions to address specific issues. It should be played at a fairly fast pace so that everybody has the chance to 'act out' a character.

Aim

To introduce the group to role-play and drama-based activities. It also enables group members to 'act out' issues, which may be relevant to them in a safe environment.

You will need

- a set of 'act out cards'
- information around issues likely to be raised through the session (e.g. bullying).

How to do it

Start the session with a short discussion about how non-verbal communication often shows others how we are feeling or behaving without any words being spoken. Ask the young people to consider how true this is and to think about their own body language.

Next, explain that you are going to ask for a volunteer to demonstrate this. Introduce the set of cards you have and the game. Tell the group that while one person is 'acting out' what is on the card, the others should ask questions to try and guess what is on the card. All questions must be answered in character so, for example, if your card says 'Being angry', you can reply to the question 'How are you?' by shouting, 'What has it got to do with you?'

If you are met with a shy silence, volunteer yourself or your co-worker to take the first turn. Often this is a great success, especially if you really over-act!

A guess can be made at any stage in the process. If it is correct, then the person who guessed takes a new card and begins again. If the guess is wrong, continue until someone gets it right. Try and keep the questions moving along so that the game keeps pace.

This should be a game that is thought provoking but good fun. Be aware that some cards may be uncomfortable for the young person who draws one to 'act out'. For example, a young person who has been the victim of a bully may not be happy to 'act out' being scared or even being a bully. You will need to be sensitive to the group's needs and, if necessary, swap cards.

ACT OUT CARDS

Being scared	Being a bully	Being bullied	Being happy
Being upset	Being proud	Being in love	Being lonely
Being hungry	Being rich	Being poor	Being kind
Being excited	Being bored	Being tired	Being silly
Being angry	Being in a big crowd	Being disappointed	Being frustrated

2.5 The mish

This introduction to role-play was told to me by a drama therapist who uses it regularly with groups of up to 12 young people. I don't know where the name comes from or what it means, but it is as it was told to me!

Aim

To introduce the concept of role-play and acting out situations to young people. It builds confidence and, because it has a built-in time boundary, it enables even the most reluctant group member to take part.

You will need

- nothing!

How to do it

Set the 'scene' that the role-play is going to take place within. If you are working in a park, you could use the 'props' you have around you such as a park bench; if you are on an estate, look for a bus shelter or a seat by the shops. This then becomes your stage area. If you cannot see anything to use, be creative and designate an area that becomes an imaginary shop or a café.

Explain to the group that everyone is going to take part in this role-play but that, apart from one person, they only have to go on 'stage' twice each. They can do this as themselves or they may want to create a character. You can increase the number of stage appearances required if you think that the group is really keen on the idea.

The remaining person holds a 'wild card' – this can be imaginary too! Holding this card enables them to go on stage as many times as they like. It is a really good idea to be selective about whom you give this to. Certainly the first time you play, it can help to give the 'wild card' to a young person who is usually quite vocal and confident!

Then make the proviso that only three members of the group can be on stage at any one time, including the 'wild card'.

Select three young people to start. If they are shy, include yourself in this. Explain that they can stay on 'stage' for as long or short a time as they wish. You may need to manage this if someone takes over!

For example, if you have chosen to set your scene in a café you may choose to be the café worker. The young person who comes in can then order a drink and talk to the next group member who comes in, and the improvisation can go on from there.

When the role-play has been taken as far as it can be the young person then returns to the rest of the group and taps another member on the shoulder who then goes on the stage. Because no one can go on the stage more than twice (apart from the 'wild card'), the session has a time boundary around it that can be very reassuring for less confident group members. The 'wild card' does not need to be chosen so can cut in at any time as long as there are no more than three people on the stage. This is often used by a group as a technique for supporting quieter members by allowing the 'wild card' to cut in.

Keep going until everybody has had a turn, and then review the process. Encourage the young people to consider how easy or hard it was to have no plot to follow, if it was easier to play a character or be themselves and how it felt to have other group members watching.

Follow-up sessions can then be planned.

2.6 The bus stop

This is another drama-based activity designed to encourage young people to engage in role-play. It works best with smaller groups of people who know each other enough to be confident in arguing their case!

Aim

To enable young people to practise formulating arguments and asserting themselves within a role-play environment.

You will need

- nothing!

How to do it

Explain to the young people that this activity revolves around a group of strangers waiting to catch a bus.

Ask the group to nominate one person to be the 'bus driver'. This should not be you or another youth worker because your role will be to facilitate what happens within the group. If you know the group, it is an idea to manage this process so that someone can experience the leadership role of bus driver who would not normally get the opportunity.

The rest of the group stands in a line, representing a bus queue. Suggest that they formulate characters for themselves that explains why they are in the bus queue. If they are looking doubtful, offer a few ideas yourself – for example, a mother carrying shopping, a man coming home from work, a student on their way back from college.

The bus driver pulls up and says to the queue, 'One place, and one place only.'

Each person in the queue then needs to present their reason for having the last place on the bus! Encourage the young people to be creative about the reasons they use to tell the bus driver why they need the place. For example, the mother may have children at home who are waiting for her to take them swimming!

Remind the young people throughout the process that the final choice lies with the bus driver who is the only one who can decide who gets the seat.

Once the decision has been made, talk the experience through with the group. Did they think it was a good decision? What else could they have said to alter the bus driver's mind? How did it feel to have one person making the decision?

2.7 Hairbraiding

This is a great way of engaging young people in conversation – it is hard for them to escape while you are holding their hair! Seriously, hairbraiding works very well in the summer with small groups of young people. We usually start by getting the braids and beads out onto a blanket, which we make the 'base' for the session. The word usually gets around and young people approach us to see if they can have a braid or learn how to do it. Once shown, the young people usually start to work alongside youth workers and finally begin to do their own braids on other members of the group.

Aim

To encourage the young people to talk with youth workers and each other. Allowing a person to braid your hair is a trust-building exercise, as is braiding someone else's. It also gives the young people a new skill to use outside the session.

You will need

- coloured embroidery threads
- scissors
- a comb
- a strong hair grip

- a mirror

- beads.

How to do it

Select a thin section of hair. Comb it through and clip back any surrounding strands.

Ask the young person to choose three different colour embroidery threads and a bead.

Plait the section of hair you have chosen for a braid.

Cut the three chosen threads into lengths. The minimum of each of these should be 3 x the length of the hair to be braided.

As tightly as you can, tie the threads around the top of the hair that you have sectioned off, leaving equal lengths either side.

Then, keeping the tension as tight as you can, hold the plait and one length of braid in one hand and 'wrap' the hair with the other three strands.

As you bind down the plait, alternate colours and which side of the plait you take the thread in. The golden rule for success is to always have three threads in your hand and three around the hair!

Once you come to the end of the hair, do not panic! This is the easy bit. Braid to the end of the hair and slightly over. Taking a set of three threads in each hand, tie the ends together. Do this a couple of times to make sure that it is secure. Thread the bead on and tie.

Cut off any loose ends and admire!

2.8 Fake tattoos

This is as fast and simple or as slow and complicated as you want. We used to use fine water-based felt pens, coloured in with face paints, but last summer we experimented with henna and this works really well.

Aim

To encourage the young people to engage with the youth workers. At its simplest this is just a fun activity, but it is also a tool to open up discussions around body art and tattoos. The henna tattoos can also be used to build cultural awareness.

You will need

- henna or fine black water-based pens

- face paints or water-based ink

- a fine paint brush
- water in a screw-top jar
- a sheet of carbon paper
- designs to choose from.

How to do it

If you are not confident at drawing freehand or want to be sure of good results, prepare before you go!

Buy some tattoo transfers. Lots of high-street shops sell them and there is a pretty good choice. Avoid anything openly aggressive, but things like dragons and hearts are always popular. Trace the designs onto tracing paper – you could enlarge them on a photocopier if you wanted – with thin black pen. These will become your templates.

1. Place the template over a small piece of carbon paper on the young person's arm. Be sensitive to gender issues here – female youth workers working with young women. Also agree boundaries as to which areas you are happy to decorate and which you are not.

2. Once you have the faint mark of the template on the skin, go over it with your pen.

3. Next get the young person to select the colours to have in the 'tattoo'. By this stage you usually have an audience!

4. Use the face paint to fill in the colour. This will last until it is washed off with soap.

5. Encourage the young people to repeat the process with other members of the group.

6. Facilitate discussions that look at tattoos and body art, including issues around attitudes and values, stereotypes and the legal age to be tattooed.

2.9 Worry beads

These beads can be made into lots of different things including earrings, anklets and necklaces.

Aim

To enable the young people to produce a bracelet of 'worry beads' by working co-operatively with their peers.

You will need

- a good selection of coloured paper, including silver and gold (this should be about 100 gsm in weight)
- glue
- thin elastic
- scissors
- knitting needles or skewers
- pens
- rulers (optional)
- spray paint (optional).

How to do it

It is usually a good idea to wear a bracelet 'you made earlier' so you can show the group the sort of thing that can be achieved. In summer we also wear them around ankles.

Divide the large group into smaller ones. If possible, no more than four should work together so each person can be at a different stage and be able to share equipment easily. This means participants will have to plan their work so that they enable each other to complete the activity.

Choose coloured paper and mark with the pen into triangles. If you want to do this really precisely, use a ruler, but you should be aiming for 16 or 18 triangles out of each sheet. Each triangle needs to be approximately 2.5 cm (1") at the base and the width of the sheet. The smaller the beads you want, the smaller the triangles you need to make. Use the scissors to cut the triangles out.

Put the large end of a triangle around a knitting needle (or skewer). Roll it up as tightly as possible and glue firmly at the point.

Hold in place until the glue sets, then pull the needle out. It should stay in place! This is one bead. Now make enough to go around your wrist.

When all the beads are ready and dry, push the elastic through the beads and tie the ends together.

At this point, if you want all your beads the same colour or to have a shiny finish, you could use spray paint.

2.10 20-minute sculptures

This can be the prelude session to a longer sculpture project or an activity in its own right. The good thing is that you need no particular artistic ability to achieve a result. It is also appropriate for young people with physical disabilities, as no small motor skills are needed.

Aim

To introduce sculpture as an art form available to anyone.

You will need

- modroc (strips of bandage pre-soaked in plaster of Paris) – cut into strips 5 cm (2") long
- Vaseline®
- scissors
- water in a screw-top jar
- plastic bowl
- newspaper
- gold or silver spray paint (optional)
- sequins (optional)
- glitter (optional)

This sounds like a lot to carry but will all fit into a carrier bag!

How to do it

Ask for a volunteer! Then ask the person to choose a hand or foot to have 'sculpted'. Cover the hand or foot with Vaseline. This is to stop the modroc sticking to any hairs or skin.

Pour the water into the plastic bowl and slowly soak a strip of plaster in the water. Immediately place this onto the volunteer's hand – it is best to start with the largest area first. Slowly cover the hand completely, including the fingers.

Once the hand is covered in several layers of modroc, wet your finger and go over the bandage smoothing it flat.

Leave to dry. This will take about ten minutes, but may be longer if you have a lot of layers. You can tell when it is dry because it starts to peel away from the hand, usually from the fingers first.

You should have a perfect cast or 'sculpture' of the young person's hand or foot. You can do it on faces but I once had an unfortunate accident with a young woman with very long hair and this has put me off a bit! Seriously, faces can be done, but it can be quite frightening for the young person to have their face completely covered in a mask. If you do decide to have a go, make sure that you have put lots of Vaseline on and scraped back all hair from the young person's face. The casts look really good sprayed gold or silver and decorated with sequins and glitter.

2.11 Grab!

This is a team game that you can play with up to 20 young people. It encourages them to develop skills to achieve a goal without using force.

Aim

To develop strategies to 'grab' the object in the middle of the group without touching any member of the opposite team – this is harder than you think!

You will need

- a small object to grab – this can be anything from your kit bag.

How to do it

Divide the group into two teams. If there is an even number, both youth workers facilitate the game; if not, one of you join a team.

Ask the two groups to stand in a line opposite each other, leaving a space of approximately 3 metres between them.

If you have 20 people, number the two teams one to ten, so that number ten stands opposite number one of the opposing team and diagonal to its number ten. This will then follow through for each number.

1	2	3	4	5	6	7	8	9	10
10	9	8	7	6	5	4	3	2	1

Place the object in the middle of the two teams.

Call numbers out between one and ten (or the highest number in the teams).

When each number is called, the corresponding young people run to the middle and attempt to 'grab' the object without touching their opposing team mate.

The team whose member is successful is awarded a point; otherwise the opposition gets the point! This game needs skill and speed. Tactics are usually developed as the game goes on.

The first team to ten points wins.

2.12 Don't fall in!

This is a team-building exercise that can be played anywhere; just be creative about the space you are going to use. The more people you have in the group, the more effort is needed on their part to complete the task. However, I think that it would not be much fun with fewer than six young people.

Aim

To encourage the young people to work together to achieve a common goal.

You will need

- nothing, except to have identified an area suitable for the game. You could use a kerbstone, if it is safe, or a railway sleeper, a low barrier or apparatus in a park. For safety reasons I would be careful about using anything too high. If you can't find anywhere, then take some chalk with you and draw a thick line to use.

How to do it

Ask the group to stand in a row along your designated area. Explain that the object of the task you are setting is for all the participants to arrange themselves along the kerb (or whatever you have chosen) in alphabetical order as fast as possible. Set a maximum time to complete this in according to the size of the group. Do not tell them what the task is going to be until they have stood in place!

There are rules to this!

1. The order is alphabetical to their first names.

2. Once everyone is in a line along the straight area, no one must touch the ground on either side throughout the task. (You can embellish this as much as you like depending on the age of the group and how well you know them. For example, the area on either side can become crocodile-infested water or quicksand!)

3. The whole group has to decide and agree before any person can move.

4. The participants can enable each other to move about.

5. The youth workers are there to facilitate, not to advise, but can intervene if any suggestion is dangerous.

Once the task has been completed, review it. How easy was it? What roles did people take? How did it feel when they were successful?

2.13 Human sculpture

This game is a good prelude for either of the next two activities, 'Trust game' and 'Trust game by the sea'. It familiarises the young people with being close to each other and begins to build trust within the group.

Aim

To encourage the young people to work together and become sensitive to each other's personal space and comfort zones.

You will need

- nothing!

How to do it

Ask the group to nominate a volunteer or, if you think this may be difficult, choose one yourself. The volunteer then moves away from the group out of sight with your co-worker.

Explain to the group that the idea is to form a 'human sculpture' that is as complicated as possible. You may want to introduce ground rules around appropriate touching and allowing people to opt out if they find the closeness too much. If this happens, they can always become an active observer to ensure that no one cheats, etc.

Once the young people have entwined themselves into as intricate a shape as possible, call back the young person who has been waiting out of sight with your co-worker. Explain that the task now is to undo the human sculpture and free everyone. Once again ask the young person to be sensitive as to how they undo the group members!

You will be surprised that this is not as easy as it seems – often the more the young person tries to undo the sculpture, the more complicated the process becomes! It usually takes about 15 minutes from start to finish and can be repeated as many times as the group wants!

2.14 Trust game

This works well with small groups of young people whom you have worked with before. It is a good way to start a session around positive relationships, friendships and building trust.

Aim

To allow members of the group to experience being the 'trusted' and the 'trusting'. It encourages them to consider how their own actions have an impact on others, and how that feels in reverse.

You will need

- to have good knowledge of the area so you can identify a space that provides a kind of 'obstacle' course for the young people to navigate

- a scarf to use as a blindfold.

How to do it

Ask the young people to nominate a volunteer. It can be good to lead this part if you feel that someone may be pressured into doing it. Explain to them that the point of this activity is to encourage them to trust each other and to take responsibility for their own actions and others' safety. Tell them that, if they feel really uncomfortable at any point in the exercise, they should say, and the group will stop.

Ask the volunteer to step forward to be blindfolded. Make sure the blindfold is working and ask the person to describe how it feels not being able to see.

Lead the young person, with eyes still covered, to the area that you have identified for the session. Choose another member of the group to lead the volunteer next. Explain that the role of the rest of the group is to support the young person who has the blindfold on.

Facilitate as the young people negotiate the course that you have chosen. Ask them to reflect on their feelings, particularly if the young person leading loses concentration or is careless in giving directions. Then reverse the process.

Alternatively, you could ask the group to work in pairs and go through the exercise, taking it in turns to lead and be led.

Ask the group for feedback when everyone has had a turn. How did it feel to be dependent on someone? Was it better to be led or to lead? Did it make a difference if you were able to choose your partner? How did it feel if your partner gave you bad information?

This can take as long as you want depending on the area that you choose for navigation.

2.15 Trust game by the sea

This is the same game as the last activity, 'Trust game', except that you need to be by the sea! For it to be really successful, you need to be focusing on a small group. Make sure you do a risk assessment before you go, and check out any potential dangers.

Aim

To provide young people with the opportunity to be both the 'trusted' and the 'trusting'. It encourages them to reflect on the different ways a similar experience can feel, depending on where you are in it.

You will need

- to have checked the area of beach you intend to use and made sure that it is safe

- a scarf to use as a blindfold.

How to do it

Explain that the idea of the exercise is to build trust between members of the group and for individuals to take responsibility for their own actions and the safety of others. One participant will wear a blindfold, and another will lead them around the beach close to the sea, taking care that no one gets wet.

Ask for a volunteer, making sure that no one is pressured into doing anything unwillingly. Set a ground rule that, if anyone feels really uncomfortable at any point in the exercise, they should say, and the group will stop.

Ask the volunteer to step forward to be blindfolded. Make sure the blindfold is working and ask the person to describe how it feels not being able to see.

Choose another member of the group to lead the volunteer. Explain that the role of the rest of the group is to support the young person who has the blindfold on.

Facilitate as the young people negotiate the beach. Ask them to reflect on their feelings, particularly if the young person leading loses concentration or is careless in giving directions. Then reverse the process.

Alternatively, you could ask the group to work in pairs and go through the exercise, taking it in turns to lead and be led.

Ask the group for feedback when everyone has had a turn. How did it feel to be dependent on someone? Was it better to be led or to lead? Did it make a difference if you were able to choose your partner? How did it feel if your partner let you get wet?

2.16 Group communication activity

Aim

To demonstrate the need for clear communication to achieve a group task. You can do this as a whole-group activity, or divide the young people into teams.

You will need

- a skipping rope or washing line
- a scarf to use as a blindfold
- a chair
- a hat
- a glass
- a jug of water.

How to do it

To prepare for the session make a set of instructions that read: 'Direct the listener to put on the hat, sit on the chair and pour a glass of water, then drink it.'

Put the rope down as a starting line and ask all the young people to stand behind it.

Ask the group to select its best listener, and invite that person to cross the rope and stand wearing the blindfold approximately 6 metres (20 feet) away from everyone else. This young person is now 'the listener' and cannot speak until the activity is over. 'The listener' is not allowed to move unless directed to once the task is underway.

Now, ask the group to select its best communicator. Bring that person forward approximately 3 metres (10 feet) to a position facing the group with 'the listener' behind. This person is now 'the communicator'. 'The communicator' may not turn around to look behind until the end of the game, but is allowed to speak. The rest of the young people should remain in a line just behind the rope.

Tell the group behind the rope that no one may say anything until the activity is over.

Now bring out the props and place them randomly in the space between 'the listener' and 'the communicator'. Hand the instructions to the group behind the rope.

Without speaking, the group has to use forms of non-verbal communication to make 'the communicator' understand the directions so that they can tell 'the listener' what to do. The rules are that 'mouthing' or whispering the directions to 'the communicator' is not permitted, and the young people cannot use anything other than what has been given to them.

Once the young people have achieved the task, review the process with them. What made it hard to communicate? What helped? Pull out the main points to refer to in a later session.

2.17 Space

This is a really good way of illustrating the concept of 'personal space'. Young people are often asked by adults to 'give them space' and this is a good way of showing them that we all have personal boundaries. It could also be used as a pre-session activity to one of the projects in the next section, such as 'Back off!'

Aim

To introduce the issue of personal space and body 'comfort zones'.

You will need

- a piece of chalk.

How to do it

Divide the group into two equal smaller groups.

Draw a chalk line at equal distances away from a centre point. If you are working in a shopping precinct, use the distance between the two sides of shops. Make sure that the area is clear of potential trip hazards!

Group 2 should now form a straight line along the chalk mark or wall that you have identified.

Ask Group 1 to move slowly towards Group 2, from the opposite side of the area, with their arms outstretched. Group 2 should stand as still as possible.

Members of Group 2 should raise their hands in front of their chests as soon as a young person from Group 1 comes uncomfortably close to them.

Once everyone has done this and all of Group 1 has a partner from Group 2, stop. Ask everyone to stay where they are and look about. The distance or 'personal space' left between each couple will vary depending on what individuals feel comfortable with.

Reflect on the experience and discuss it with the group. The activity can then lead on to work around keeping safe and protective behaviour.

2.18 Edible art

I have never worked with a group that did not enjoy this art form! You can make it as intricate as possible, competitive or thematic depending on the age of the group. It really works best with small groups of young people under the age of 14. However, depending on how good your sweet selection is, you may encourage older groups to participate!

Aim

To encourage creativity and the sharing of resources.

You will need

- a good selection of small sweets, jellies, marshmallows, sugar bootlaces etc.
- different coloured small tubes of soft icing
- rice paper sheets
- margarine tubs or small containers.

How to do it

If you have a group larger than six, split them into two smaller groups. Divide the 'art materials' into the small pots and place a selection within each group. Before you hand out the rice paper, set a few ground rules so that the especially hungry members of the group do not swipe all the sweets!

Encourage the young people to plan their design, stressing that the object is to be creative and not to place as many sweets as possible onto the paper. You could set a theme to give the young people some ideas, or tie it in with issue-based work. Some young people I worked with produced some really effective red ribbon designs for AIDS Awareness Day.

Once everybody has finished, ask the young people to display their pieces of work. Encourage the group members in turn to explain what each pattern or picture represents, and what it means to them.

Finally, give the go-ahead for the groups to eat their art!

2.19 Cooking with candles

You will need to do a risk assessment before you decide whether to try this out. The composition of the group and how well you know the young people will be a major factor, but this is an easy and fun experience.

Aim

To enable the young people to cook something outside that they are able to share.

You will need

- batter – in a water-tight container
- small container of cooking oil
- caster sugar
- tea lights
- matches
- a large spoon
- napkins
- a flat knife or small spatula
- large, empty, clean tin cans with the lids completely removed and holes punched into the sides
- tea towels (for lifting hot tins).

Batter recipe

- 125 g (4½ oz.) plain flour
- pinch of salt
- two teaspoons caster sugar
- one egg
- 300 ml (10 fl oz.) milk
- 25 g (1 oz.) melted butter or margarine.

Put the dry ingredients into a bowl. Make a well in the centre and add the egg and half the milk. Slowly mix together to make a thick batter. Stir in the rest of the milk and melted butter. Beat for 2 or 3 minutes. Place in the water-tight container and put in the fridge until you are ready to go out.

How to do it

Make up the batter recipe in advance.

Light the tea lights and set them onto a flat area (paving slabs are good for this).

Place the large tin cans over the tea lights. The number of these you set up will depend on the size of the group. You should be able to see the candlelight through the holes. If you do not make the holes, the candle will go out – it needs oxygen to circulate.

Give the cans about 5 minutes to really heat up. Resist the temptation to touch them to see of they are ready!

Place a small amount of the oil on the top of the heated surface of one of the tin cans.

When the oil starts to bubble, use the spoon to put a thin layer of the batter onto the cooking surface.

When it begins to set, gently use the spatula or knife to turn the pancake over. This is not an exact science, but the hit and miss nature of it is part of the fun!

When it is ready, take the pancake off the tin can and place on a napkin ready to sprinkle sugar on and eat!

Continue with each member of the group taking a turn at being the 'chef' until all the batter has gone.

2.20 Chocolate game

This works well with groups of up to ten young people. Although it is particularly popular with younger groups, anyone who likes chocolate is usually more than happy to play!

Aim

To give the young people and youth workers an equal chance of being successful in obtaining as much chocolate as possible!

You will need

- a large bar of chocolate that you have left in the fridge until the last possible moment to get it as cold as you can

- a knife and fork

- a die

- a hat, scarf and gloves

- a tray

- a scarf to use as a blindfold (optional).

How to do it

Ask the young people to sit in as wide a circle as they can make. The chocolate is placed on the tray in the middle of the circle with the knife and fork, hat, scarf and gloves. The workers should sit within the group.

Explain the rules:

1. Take turns to throw the die. If you throw a six, go into the centre of the circle and put on the hat, scarf and gloves. With the knife and fork you are now free to eat as much chocolate as you can before somebody else throws a six. If this does not sound hard enough, you can use a blindfold too.

2. If you use your hands, you lose your turn and have to return to the circle!

3. The moment the next six is thrown, you must stop, put the props down and go back to the circle.

4. This carries on until all the chocolate has been eaten!

Encourage the group to support whomever is in the middle while they try and secure some chocolate.

2.21 Quick photos

This is a really effective and easy activity. The main drawback is that you need some daylight to get clear results so there are restrictions on when you can do it. You can often pick up out-of-date paper cheaply from commercial photographers or college art departments, and it will be fine for this activity.

Aim

To introduce young people to the basic principles of photography.

You will need

- black and white photographic paper (kept in the box)

- Vaseline

- developer

- fixer

- a screw-top bottle of water

- two photographic trays

- tongs.

How to do it

The easiest way to get young people interested in this is to demonstrate it yourself first.

Smear a thin layer of Vaseline on your hand. You could also do this on the sole of your foot if it is summer, or on your face if you are very brave!

Making sure that you keep the rest of the paper in the protective packaging and box, remove a sheet of photographic paper. Immediately place your Vaselined hand into the middle of the paper and leave for a couple of seconds.

Put the paper face down into one of the trays filled with developer. Remove from the developer with tongs and you will see a very basic 'photo' begin to appear on the paper. Dip it into the tray of fixer for one minute and then wash it briefly in water.

You can get some good results with this if you make a collage, where several of the group place their hands together on the paper. You could also experiment with flowers, leaves, etc. Leave to dry.

2.22 Break the code

This is a really excellent teambuilding activity, but you do need to plan it well in advance. It is great fun to do at night, but you should ask the young people to bring torches with them and you should be prepared to do a risk assessment in advance.

Aim

To encourage young people to work together in teams to achieve a common goal.

You will need

- to research the area and devise a sheet of instructions or questions based on local landmarks and sites (copy one for each group)

- a risk assessment

- two torches

- pens

- four boxes, each with a small chain and combination padlock holding it shut

- four keys for the padlocks.

How to do it

BEFORE THE SESSION

Plan your instructions. These should be simple and based on the local area. All the answers should lead to numerical solutions that in turn will be the combinations that you set on the padlocks. For example, 'Walk to the end of the road and turn left. When you get to the bus shelter look up. Write down the middle number of the first line of numbers…'

Prepare a box for each group. Place tissue paper and glitter inside and secure the box with a chain and combination padlock. You could put sweets, shredded newspaper or anything you want into the box.

AT THE SESSION

Meet up with the young people and divide them into four groups. Explain that each group is going to be given a 'gunge bomb' to hold. Tell them that the only way to diffuse it is to break the code on the combination padlock holding the box shut. You can be as dramatic as you like over this bit depending on the group!

Give out the instruction sheet and explain that by following the clues each group should be able to solve the puzzle. Tell them that each group will be timed and will be competing against each other to diffuse the 'gunge bomb' fastest. Finally, agree a meeting place where the youth workers will stay holding the keys. This is where the groups should come to when they think that they have broken the code.

1. Send each of the groups off 5 minutes apart.

2. Make sure that one of the workers circulates around the area to support the groups and to see that there are no problems.

3. Once the first group members return to the meeting place, they are allowed one go at defusing the 'grunge bomb'.

4. If they are successful, check their time and register it. If not, send them off again.

5. Once all the groups have returned and opened their boxes, check the times. The group that completed the task in the fastest time 'wins'.

6. Review the process with the group.

2.23 Three words

Aim

To develop communication and improvisation skills as young people work together to be creative.

You will need

- three cards for each group with the words 'WHY', 'SORRY' and 'NO' written on them
- flipchart paper and marker pens (optional).

How to do it

Break the large group into smaller ones of up to five young people. Next, hand out the word cards; each group is given the same three words, but don't tell them this at this stage.

Each group now has ten minutes to come up with a short role-play or drama scene that must include each of the three words, at least once. This will be performed and each member of the group MUST have a role. As the facilitator, be aware that having a role does not necessarily mean acting, but leave the group to work this out for themselves if it is an issue. Offer the flipchart paper and marker pens to anyone who wants to plan the scene in words first.

Invite each group to perform its sketch, and lead a round of applause after each performance. Finally, review the group process. Did anyone take the lead in planning the scene? How did 'leaders' get the others to agree with their ideas? Was there anyone reluctant to take part? Did this slow the task down? How did the rest of the group encourage that person to join in?

2.24 Sand holes

This is another activity for youth workers based on a beach. You will need to check out local tide information and complete a risk assessment before you decide whether to go ahead.

Aim

To encourage small groups of young people to work together to achieve a task.

You will need

- a risk assessment
- lots of sand
- a large black plastic bin liner.

How to do it

Ask the young people to form groups of up to four. You can do it with smaller groups, but the young people have to work harder!

When they have formed teams, issue each team with a bin liner. Explain that the aim of the activity is to complete the task as quickly as possible. They will need to work together effectively to do this.

Then explain the task:

1. The participants in each group need to dig a large, deep hole with their hands. They can do this together or in turns. Encourage them to reflect on the process as they take part.

2. When the hole is large enough for the smallest member of the group to get in, stop!

3. That person then gets inside the hole, using the black plastic bag to keep dry.

4. The rest of the group then need to fill in the hole – with the person still inside – making sure that no sand is left on the side.

5. The first group to complete the task successfully gets to choose the next activity.

6. Evaluate the process. How easy was it to work together? How did you decide roles? Who made decisions?

2.25 Halloween lanterns

This is a good activity in its own right, but it also gives the group a central point to meet around and some light to continue with other games once it is complete. You could make similar lights with other vegetables, such as turnips, at other times of the year or for barbecues.

Aim

To encourage the group to work together to produce lanterns.

You will need

- pumpkins
- strong spoons
- a sharp knife
- plastic bags
- tea lights
- matches
- string.

How to do it

Bring as many pumpkins as you can carry! Seriously, because they are heavy, try and aim for one pumpkin to about four young people. If you are working with a small group, this will be easier.

Decide whether you want the group to use the knife, or, if they are younger, delegate this duty to your co-worker. Either way, you need to cut off the top of the pumpkin about 5 cm (2") down. This will form the lid.

Scoop out all the pumpkin flesh. This is hard work so encourage the entire group to participate in this bit. Make sure you leave about 2 cm (¾") on the inside and take care not to stick the spoon straight through the skin. Put all the seeds and discarded flesh into a plastic bag for disposal later.

Carefully cut out triangular shapes for eyes, nose and mouth – the scarier the better!

Place the tea lights inside the pumpkin. These are better than candles and will stop the problem of the candle falling over as the lantern is carried.

With a matchstick, make a small hole either side of the lantern face, about 5 cm (2") below the lid. Thread string through to form a handle.

Light the tea lights and use two matches to secure the lid to the pumpkin. Gather round to tell each other ghost stories if you dare!

2.26 Festive candles

This combines candles with sweets and is always really popular, particularly with younger groups.

Aim

To celebrate with the young people you are working with on the street. This could be Christmas, Chinese New Year, birthdays or the end of a project.

You will need

- oranges
- cocktail sticks
- raisins
- soft sweets, marshmallows, etc.
- birthday cake candles
- birthday cake candleholders
- silver and gold sticky stars
- matches.

How to do it

Give each young person an orange. If more than you expected turn up, ask them to work in pairs.

Stick the gold and silver stars randomly on the orange. You could use other shapes and colours, but the silver and gold sparkles in the candlelight effectively.

Push the birthday cake candleholder into the middle of the top of the fruit. This marks the place the candle will go.

Hand around the cocktail sticks. Make sure that no one in the group decides to use these to stick other people with! Show the young people how to place the sweets, raisins and marshmallows on the end of the sticks and then push the opposite end into the orange. You can do a healthy version of this using all fruit and vegetables.

When you have plenty of 'spikes' in your orange, place the candle in the holder and light! The lights look effective placed together in the middle of the group and can then be taken home or eaten.

2.27 Egyptian art activity

This 'wax-resist' activity is based on Egyptian hieroglyphics. You can use it like this or as part of larger project around world art or cultural heritage. It is easy to do, requires little preparation and works on the basic premise that oil-based products and water do not mix. Be careful not to buy crayons that are water soluble.

Aim

To open up discussions around tagging, street art and graffiti.

You will need

- large sheets of paper
- assorted colour wax crayons
- black ink
- paintbrushes, water pots and water (in empty screw-top bottles)
- copies of the hieroglyphic alphabet.[1]

How to do it

Start by suggesting that tagging and using symbols for names is nothing new. Show the young people the hieroglyphic alphabet and invite them to guess the modern-day letters each of the symbols represents.

Now hand out sheets of paper and suggest the young people write their names using the hieroglyphics with wax crayons. Make sure that they use really dense areas of colour or it won't work.

Once the designs are complete, hand out black ink and brushes.

Thickly paint over the coloured wax, making sure brushstrokes go in one direction and no white paper is left showing through.

As the ink settles into the paper, it will 'resist' the wax areas leaving the design contrasting brightly out of the wax.

---

1   Available at www.artyfactory.com/egyptian_art/egyptian_hieroglyphs/hieroglyphs.htm, accessed on 11 August 2010.

2.28 Quick tie-dye

Aim

This is a fast activity that gives effective instant results. It needs little preparation so is great for use in detached or mobile settings. Because it is cheap to do, the young people can do lots, experimenting with colours and patterns before displaying them all together.

You will need

- a pack of thick baby wipes
- rubber bands (in a variety of thicknesses)
- watercolour marker pens
- scissors
- latex gloves.

How to do it

Hand out the baby wipes – one each to start off with so they don't dry before they are worked on. Place the rubber bands in the middle of the group and ask the young people to choose up to four.

Explain that they need to tie the bands as tightly as possible around different sections of the baby wipe. Once the young people have got the idea of this, introduce different techniques such as making a concertina out of the baby wipe and tying the bands or folding it diagonally to make different patterns.

Give everyone a pair of latex gloves to protect their hands from getting stained.

From the large selection of watercolour marker pens you have made available, invite the young people to select colours and show them how to colour the baby wipes – pressing the marker pens hard so that the ink will go all the way through the cloth. If you start with a pale colour, such as yellow, you can build through orange to red to get a graduated effect.

Using the scissors, cut through the rubber bands and unfold the cloth. There you have it – instant tie-dye! Either put them up as they are (they look good hung from trees on a bright day) or mount them onto pieces of card and put them together to make a group display.

2.29 Team shove it!

Aim

This is a competitive game that encourages young people to work together in teams.

You will need

- six coins for each team
- paper
- pens
- a watch
- Blu-Tack.

How to do it

Divide the group into teams of three and give each team six coins each to play with.

Explain that the six coins are now team 'ships' for the purpose of the game. The first task is to design a team logo to go onto a 'sail' for each ship so that teams can identify their 'fleet' of ships during the game. The sails are made by folding small pieces of paper into triangles, securing them to the coins with Blu-Tack.

Next, clear a large, flat space (concrete is best for this) and set each team up around it. In turn, each team 'shoves' one of its coins into a space on the table, using the edge of the hand. Only one shove is allowed each turn.

The idea is for the young people to get all their coins into an area for their team, so, if there are other coins for opposing teams in the way, the player should try and move these out of the way.

Allow up to 15 minutes for the game – the team with all its coins in the correct team area wins.

2.30 Building bridges

Aim

To show the roles that people take to complete a task.

You will need (for each group)

- clear sticky tape
- newspapers

- a glue stick

- scissors

- a toy car

- a list of rules

- paper and a pen

- a prize (optional).

How to do it

Divide the main group into teams of up to ten young people. Distribute the equipment listed to each group by placing one item in front of each person (the newspapers can be given to more than one person). Make sure one person in the group is given no equipment, and ask another young person to sit outside the activity and act as an observer of the process. The observer will record everything done as the group completes the task.

Explain that the group task is to build the longest newspaper bridge that will hold the car and allow it to travel from one side to the other. However, there are rules. Give these verbally:

1. No one must speak for the duration of the activity.

2. The car must be able to travel unaided across the bridge.

Write these rules out in advance and place them in the middle of the group:

1. You can only use the equipment provided.

2. You cannot take equipment from each other.

3. No gestures, hand signals or mimes.

Allow ten minutes for the groups to complete the task, circulating and strictly enforcing rules as you go! Call time and in turn invite each group to race its car across the bridge. Congratulate the team with the longest bridge that manages to get its car across, and lead a round of applause.

Now, invite the observers to feedback to their teams. What behaviour did they see? Did a leader emerge? How did that happen? Was there a turning point in the task where everyone worked together? Was anyone left out?

Bring the groups back together to reflect on the experience. In particular ask, the young people to consider why they followed any leader who emerged in their group. What qualities did they have? Was anyone in the group resentful of their power? Reinforce the idea that leaders need followers. It is the followers who give the leader power. Finally, ask them all to quietly reflect on their own roles within their groups and the contributions that they made or didn't make.

2.31 Storytime

This 'story' is told like a fairy tale but depicts a scenario that poses questions that are open to interpretation and value judgements. It works with any age and provokes the most discussion in mixed gender groups!

Aim

To open up a discussion around a series of events that highlight love, friendship and betrayal. The story itself is imaginary, but the young people are encouraged to reflect the issues into their own lives and reach conclusions.

You will need

- a copy of the 'storytime' sheet to read from.

How to do it

Ask the young people to form a circle or gather together in one group so that they can all hear you.

Introduce 'storytime' – we usually use the old 'Are you sitting comfortably? Well, then I'll begin…' routine, but it will depend on your group how you do this.

Encourage the young people to listen carefully for the twists in the story and each character's part in the events.

Once you have finished reading, pose the question 'So, whose fault is it that the baroness is dead?'

Question observations made and accusations of blame. For example, 'It was her own fault for disobeying her husband!' can be challenged to raise issues around the right of a man to threaten his wife with punishment for disobedience. Explore attitudes – What about the lover? The friend? Who should have offered help in their opinion? Facilitate a discussion that encompasses some of the points raised. This should also enable youth workers to identify any further issue-based work.

STORYTIME

Once upon a time, in a place a long way from here, a jealous baron kissed his wife goodbye as he left her to visit his other castles. 'Do not leave the castle while I am gone,' he said. 'If you do, I will punish you severely when I return!'

As the hours passed, the young baroness grew sad and lonely. Finally, she felt so alone that she decided to disobey her husband's orders and leave the castle to visit her lover who lived in the forest nearby.

Now, the castle was situated on an island in a wide, fast-flowing river, and there was only way to reach the mainland. This was to cross the drawbridge that linked the island to the forest at the narrowest part of the river.

The baroness stood at the edge of the river, 'Surely my husband will not return before dawn?' she thought. 'I will have time to visit my lover and get back before him.' With that she ordered her servants to lower the drawbridge and leave it down until she returned.

Having spent several happy hours with her lover, the baroness returned to the castle only to find that the drawbridge was blocked by a gateman. The gateman was fiercely waving a long cruel knife and shouted, 'Do not attempt to cross this bridge, Baroness, or I will have to kill you – it is the Baron's orders!'

Fearing for her life, the baroness ran back to her lover and asked him to help her. 'But our relationship is only a romantic one,' he explained. 'I thought you knew that? I will not help!'

The baroness ran back to the river and, having told her story to the boatman, pleaded for his help.

'I will do it,' said the boatman, 'but only if you can pay my fee of five marks.'

'Five marks?' exclaimed the baroness, 'but all my money is in the castle! I can pay you later.'

'Hard luck! No money, no ride,' said the boatman flatly and turned away.

Her fear growing, the baroness ran crying to her friend and, after explaining her desperate situation, begged for enough money to pay the boatman.

The friend shook her head, 'If you had not disobeyed your husband, this would not have happened. I will give you no money!'

With the sun rising behind the island and her last attempt to get help refused, the baroness returned sadly to the gate, where she was slain by the gateman as she attempted to reach the castle.

2.32 Circle game

You will need a large group to play this game effectively, but you could adapt it to work with fewer than 12 young people by placing one person at a time in the middle and moving the circle around them.

Aim

To develop confidence in role-play. It is also a good way of encouraging the group to work with members they may not usually choose to partner.

You will need

- a set of 'circle game cards'.

How to do it

Make sure that you have enough space to make a large circle before the young people arrive. As the group come together, hand each member a card. Ask each person to read it, keeping the information on it secret.

With the young people, form two circles, one inside the other. Each person needs to be facing a partner from the inner circle. Then place yourself in the middle of the group.

Ask the young people to read the cards they hold and begin conversations with the people opposite them in character. For example, one group member may hold a card saying, 'You are out on the pull tonight', and begin a conversation with the person opposite whose card says, 'You have just received a parking ticket.' Explain that the participants should not tell what their cards say, but their partners can guess. Stress that it does not matter if they get it wrong – the aim is to interact with each other.

Explain that each time you clap your hands everyone should place their cards on the ground in front of them and move to their left. This will give them all new partners and different cards each move.

The game ends when all members of the group have worked their way around the circle!

CIRCLE GAME CARDS

You have just had an argument with your best friend	You have just won £50 in a competition	It is your birthday today
You are out on the pull tonight	Your bike has just been stolen	You have just failed your driving test
The doorman has refused to let you in the club	You have just received a parking ticket	Your boyfriend has been secretly seeing your mate
You have a really bad headache	You cannot hear anyone because you are listening to your MP3 player	You are really hungry and the person opposite you has a hamburger
You need a lift home and the person opposite has a car	Your mum has unfairly grounded you for a month	You have just received your tickets to go to Ibiza this summer
You can't remember the name of the person you are speaking to	You need to borrow money off the person opposite you	You have just been offered the Saturday job you applied for

You are in a job interview	You are feeling really bored	You have forgotten that you have an exam today and you have not revised
You are home 2 hours late and need an excuse	You are in a club at the bar	You are at a football match
You think you are being followed on your way home	You are taking part in a fashion show	You are offering to help an elderly person cross the road
You have just been given the wrong change	You have just missed your train home	You are talking to someone you really fancy
You are talking to your mum's friends	You have just found a kitten and you want to keep it	Your girlfriend has just dumped you

2.33 The dinner party

This game is an introduction to group work that develops negotiation skills and the ability to compromise. You can use it with one small group or divide a larger group into fours.

Aim

To get the group to agree on six 'guests' to invite for an imaginary dinner. Guests can only go on the invite list if the whole group agrees.

You will need

- flipchart paper onto which you have already drawn a large oblong to represent the table for each group
- a watch
- spare paper
- marker pens.

How to do it

Working in groups of no more than four, set the young people the task of drawing up the guest list for the best dinner party ever! Explain that:

1. The dinner table can only seat six.

2. Guests can be chosen from anyone living or dead.

3. There should be a fairly even gender balance.

4. The young people must have reasons why the guest has been chosen that they can share.

5. All group members must agree the invite.

Hand each group a flipchart sheet with the table layout on, marker pens and a spare sheet for working out the guest list on.

Allow 20 minutes for the group to suggest, negotiate and agree their 'dinner party'.

When each group has made and agreed its final decisions, ask for a volunteer from each group to introduce the dinner party list.

Each group then shares its table plan and explains the reasons why these people have been chosen. For example, 'We agreed to invite Will Smith because he is really funny and we think that he would make everyone laugh.'

Review the process. How easy was it to agree guests? What method did the group use to reach consensus? Are there any guests who make it onto more than one list? What about those who nearly made it? Were there any criteria that made a person ineligible?

Chapter 3

Projects

3.1 How assertive are you?

The next two activities, 'What is bullying?' and 'What is healthy eating?', can be used together to begin to explore bullying and self-esteem with young people. You can use them with either young men or women, although you may want to alter the questions slightly. However, I have found that it works best with small groups of people who know each other well enough to be honest.

Aim

To look at the differences between being 'assertive' and 'aggressive', and provoke discussion within the group.

You will need

- enough copies of the 'how assertive are you? quiz' for all the group
- pens.

How to do it

Hand out a pen and a copy of the quiz to each of the young people. Explain that you want them to work on their own to begin with but, if you know that some group members will struggle with this, suggest working in pairs.

Introduce the quiz by saying that there are a series of situations and possible responses shown on the page. You want the participants to look at them and tick the responses that they feel would be closest to their own reactions in similar circumstances. Most young people are familiar with quizzes such as this in magazines, and will need minimum support at this stage.

Once they have all finished and are happy with their responses to each question, ask the group to come together.

Read out the questions and the answers and ask the young people to keep a tally of how many a's, b's and c's they have ticked as you go through the sheet.

Finally, ask them to count and see which letter they have ticked most. Then ask them to refer to the sheet to see where those answers fit. Stress that they do not need to share this analysis unless they feel comfortable doing so.

Encourage feedback and ask the young people questions around what they ticked and why, in order to provoke further discussion. Do they agree with the quiz? Is saying, 'Please don't do it' really submissive? How could they be generally more assertive and make their feelings known without being aggressive? What are the advantages and disadvantages of each response?

How assertive are you? – answers

MAINLY A

These reactions are 'submissive'; you don't always need to go along with everyone else! There is nothing wrong with being you and making your feelings and opinions known. You need to look at ways to give clearer messages that reflect what you really want.

MAINLY B

You are comfortable with being 'assertive', while remaining sensitive to other people's needs. You expect people to respect who you are and offer respect back. Make sure that you maintain this even when things get difficult!

MAINLY C

Steady there! You will find that people are more ready to listen to your point of view if you give them space and look at other ways to get your message across rather than getting angry and loud. You may be right, but no one will listen if you don't calm down!

HOW ASSERTIVE ARE YOU? QUIZ

Look at the situations and responses below. Some are 'aggressive', some are 'submissive' and some are 'assertive'. Which one sounds most like you?

1. You are standing in a queue for the bus and someone pushes in front of you. Do you:

    a) Say nothing – they may have a go at you.

    b) Tap them on the shoulder and politely explain to them where the back of the queue is.

    c) Shove past them when the bus arrives and stare hard at them if they look like saying something.

2. You are at the hairdresser's and she doesn't cut your fringe straight. Do you:

    c) Refuse to pay and have a loud argument with the stylist; after all, she is supposed to be a professional.

    a) Manage to get outside before you burst into tears – you're going to have to wear a hat for ages.

    b) Ask the stylist to check if your fringe is straight as it looks wrong to you – if you are right, you will ask her to straighten it.

3. Your best mate wants to go to a club that is open until 3am – your mum says you have to be in at midnight, but your friend wants to stay all night. Do you:

    a) Go, although you know you won't enjoy it because you have promised your mum, but she is your friend…

    b) Explain to her that you have given your mum your word, but you will go with her until you need to leave – if she is your friend, she will respect your promise too.

    c) Tell her that no one tells you what to do and get home at 5am – you can handle your mum.

4. You are with a friend whom you know has been shoplifting around the town at weekends. Suddenly in the supermarket she suggests you have a go too. You say 'No' but she keeps on pushing you. Do you:

    c) Shout, 'When I say "no", I mean "no"' and threaten to hit her if she keeps on.

b) Take her to one side and quietly say, 'When I say "no", I mean "no",' then walk away.

a) Say 'I'm sorry, I can't do it, please don't be angry with me' – you don't want to lose your friend.

5. You go to the cinema and your date suggests you see a film that you know you will hate. Do you say:

a) 'Oh all right, I don't mind going if you want to,' even though you hate action movies and really wanted to see something else.

b) 'I really don't want to see this film – can't we choose one we both like? You can always see this with your friends another time.'

c) 'No way am I going in to see that! If you insist, you can go on your own!'

6. You are walking down the corridor at school and two people from your class laugh as you go past. Do you:

c) Turn around, walk back and confront them – who do they think they are laughing at?

a) Turn around where you are and say, 'Please don't laugh at me like that, I don't like it.'

b) Walk back to where they are standing to check out if they are laughing at you and then tell them to stop, you've had enough.

7. You buy a top from a shop, but when you get home you notice it has a button missing. Do you:

a) Ask your mum to take it back – how embarrassing!

b) Take it back with the receipt the next day and ask for an exchange.

c) Go back in with all your mates and let rip about the rubbish they are trying to sell – that will teach them!

8. At the youth club all your mates are slagging off one of the CDs being played – it's yours! Do you:

b) Own up – you don't care, you think it's great.

a) Laugh along with the rest and hope that the youth worker doesn't hand it back to you while they're looking.

c) Feel really angry and start an argument – who is criticising you now?

3.2 What is bullying?

This activity encourages the young people you are working with to begin to think about the different forms that bullying can take. It can be used with the 'How assertive are you? quiz' to form part of an ongoing project around self-image and personal esteem.

Aim

To offer a starting point for young people to discuss bullying and the effects that it has on both the victim and the bully.

You will need

- two sets of the 'what is bullying? cards'
- contact numbers and leaflets for local support groups.

How to do it

In two groups, ask the young people to read the set of cards you are handing out. Explain that both groups will have the same information on their cards.

Then ask them to assess each of the situations outlined on the cards and, as a group, agree whether they depict a bullying situation or not. You will need to be sensitive to any young person within the group whom you suspect or know has been a victim of bullying.

When the young people have had a chance to discuss the situations and reach agreement, bring everybody together in a large group.

Read out each of the cards and ask the two groups what they decided. Is it the same? Facilitate a discussion over each card – what could the young people have done if they were being bullied? What would they do if it happened to them? Why do they think people become bullies? Discuss protective tactics and strategies for being assertive in bullying situations. Make sure that the young people have information and contact numbers for support, including someone to tell if they feel that they are actual or potential victims.

WHAT IS BULLYING? CARDS

'I have told her before, the reason I shout is so I don't hit her... I can't say fairer than that, can I?'	'Ben says that if I want him to keep quiet about it I have to give him my dinner money all of next week.'
'Miss Betts always picks on me – she knows I don't have the answer but she likes making me cry in front of the class.'	'The boss at my Saturday job keeps putting his arms round me when he shows me how to work the till – it is really revolting.'
'I like football but we have to get off the pitch when the older boys come out.'	'My dad always asks me to do the washing up – never my brother.'
'Zoë says that if I want a boyfriend I had better lose some weight and get rid of my spots.'	'My boyfriend says that if I love him I will stay at his house when his parents are away – I am scared.'
'Kelly keeps following me about, I try ignoring her but she won't get the hint.'	'Every time I walk past Mark and his mates they all laugh at me and call me "Shorty".'
'If she wants to come out with me she will have to lend me her new top, otherwise she can go on her own.'	'That bus driver always shouts at us when we get on his bus – last night he only let half of us on.'

'Have you seen Daryl in PE? What a sight, we all laugh as he comes into the gym!'	'Like maths? No way! I don't want everyone thinking that I am a boffin.'
'I have tried ignoring them, but they just throw things at my back as I walk into youth club.'	'I like Daniel, but all my friends will laugh if I go out with him.'
'So I told him, "Go out with you? No way" – he would probably want his mummy to come too!'	'It is hard, every time I come out of school one of them is there waiting for me.'

3.3 What is healthy eating?

This exercise has been used with groups as an introductory session to look at body image. It can be supported with leaflets on diet and fitness as appropriate. Any topics or concerns raised during the session can be identified for further work.

Aim

To raise the issue of healthy eating in a non-confrontational way, and to open up discussions around lifestyle choices.

You will need

- magazines
- scissors
- marker pens
- glue sticks
- flipchart paper.

How to do it

Split the group into two. Set one group the task of looking through the magazines and finding examples of healthy images, the other the task of finding unhealthy images. Explain that these can be of food, people or activities.

Then ask each group to take its images and make them into a collage on the flipchart paper. Agree that it is OK to supplement the cuttings with words, slogans or feelings written with the marker pens.

Bring the two groups back together to share their collages.

Ask questions to prompt discussion:

1. How easy was it to find unhealthy options?

2. Are there any stereotypes?

3. What is the major difference between the people shown in each collage?

Then ask the participants to look at their own eating habits. Ask them all to think of one healthy option they could choose to introduce to their lifestyle for the next week. This could be giving up smoking, cutting out sugar, limiting chocolate or walking to school. The youth workers will need to make a pledge too! Do try and encourage the young people to make realistic goals so that they can feel good about achieving them if they succeed, but not too embarrassed to come back if they don't!

Record the pledges onto a sheet and keep for next week.

3.4 Food quiz

This quiz builds on the work started in the 'What is healthy eating?' collage and encourages young people to think about what they eat.

Aim

To give basic, correct information for young people to begin to make informed choices about the diet they eat.

You will need

- copies of the 'food quiz'
- pens
- support leaflets and information (in case the session raises questions you can't answer).

How to do it

Hand out a copy of the 'food quiz' to each group member. If you know that some members have difficulties with written exercises, encourage them to work in pairs.

Allow about 15 minutes for them to look at the questions and consider their answers. Ask them to work individually or in pairs without reference to other members at this stage.

Go through the questions and answers with the group, discussing responses.

Food quiz – Answers

1, No; 2, No; 3c; 4c; 5, Yes; 6d; 7, No; 8c; 9b; 10c; 11b; 12a; 13, No; 14b; 15a; 16, No.

FOOD QUIZ

1. A 'grab' pack of crisps has as many calories as a sandwich.　　Yes/No

2. Starchy foods are particularly fattening.　　Yes/No

3. How many spoons of sugar are in a can of cola?

   a) 4　　　　b) 1　　　　c) 7　　　　d) 8

4. Which of these foods contains the most fibre?

   a) crisps　　　b) low-fat yoghurt　　　c) baked beans

5. Frozen vegetables are as good for you as fresh.　　Yes/No

6. How many pieces of fruit and vegetables should you eat a day to stay healthy?

   a) 2　　　b) 3　　　c) 4　　　d) 5　　　e) 6　　　f) 7

7. Skimmed milk has less calcium than full fat.　　Yes/No

8. Which is the healthiest way to eat potatoes?

   a) boiled　　b) chips　　c) jacket　　d) roast

9. Which cheese has the most fat in it?

   a) Edam　　b) Cheddar　　c) cottage cheese

10. What should you do to eat a more healthy diet?

    a) cut out sweets and chocolate

    b) cut down on dairy products

    c) cut down on all fat and eat more fibre – bread, pasta, rice

11. Which drink should you increase to become healthier?

    a) fruit juice　b) water　　c) diet fizzy drinks

12. If food says that it is 'organic', it means:

    a) that it has been produced without pesticides or genetic modification

    b) that it has been grown locally

    c) that it is not as good as the usual type of fruit and vegetables

    d) that you can only buy it in healthfood shops

13. Butter has more calories than margarine.   Yes/No

14. Which of these foods contains the least fat?

   a) digestive biscuit   b) slice of bread   c) packet of low-fat crisps

15. If you want to stay healthy you should:

   a) exercise more and eat less fat

   b) eat foods marked 'low fat'

   c) cut out breakfast

   d) never eat chips

16. You have to put sugar on food to give yourself energy.   Yes/No

3.5 Living here – video diary

To make this project work, you need to be very clear with the young people that, although the intention is to highlight the local needs of young people, the video alone may not ensure that these are met. However, it is a good way of letting local community groups or parish councils see that young people do have views and can make them heard in a positive way.

Aim

To find out from the young people what they think the issues are for their areas, and to encourage the group to look at positive ways to make their voices heard by decision makers. You will also need to have basic information to hand about how decisions are made locally.

You will need

- five sessions
- a camcorder – make sure you charge the battery and take a spare along!
- paper and pens to plan interview questions on and record information
- 'activity consent forms' if you decide to 'go public' with your video.

How to do it

SESSION 1

Ask the young people to think about the area that they live in. Encourage them to consider:

1. Why they meet on the street?
2. What is there for young people to do in their neighbourhood?
3. If they were in charge of the local council, what would they change to help young people?

Discuss the issues raised within the group and agree the main ones to focus on. Also ask the participants to consider who they think should be listening to them.

Then ask them to nominate and agree a camera person, director, interviewers and interviewees. Explain what each role is and how by working together they can make a short film. These roles can be rotated so everyone has the opportunity of different experiences.

The interviewers then work together to decide questions to ask the others. The interviewees need to decide locations, etc. One of the best to date was shot entirely in a bus shelter! The camera operator and director can then make a storyboard and decide the order to shoot.

SESSION 2

Review last session's work. Are they all happy with their roles? Are any adjustments needed?

Go through the questions and answers a few times so that the young people are comfortable with the questions and have thought about their answers.

Encourage them to take the filming slowly, shooting the agreed scenes. Use the playback on the video camera for instant feedback as to how it is looking. You can also edit on some cameras. When the young people are happy that their message has got across, stop!

Now discuss what they want to happen next. If they agree that they want to take the project further and show it publicly, you will need to obtain 'activity consent forms'. If the young people are under 18, these will need to be from parents or carers; over 18s can give consent themselves. Hand out the forms and stress that these will need to be completed and handed back to the youth workers at the next session.

Ask the group to think about a suitable venue to show the video.

SESSION 3

Before this session happens, you have time to look at the video and check it for sound and clarity. Any glaring problems can either be edited or re-shot at the next session. You can then let the group members see what they did at the last session.

Collect in all the 'activity consent forms'. It is really important to have these and to be prepared to answer any questions that carers or parents may have.

With the young people, identify likely places or groups to show the video too. Parish and town councils may be a good place to start, or local residents' associations.

Discuss the group that is chosen and what its role is in local decisions. Support the young people in writing a letter to introduce themselves and the project they have worked on.

SESSION 4

Show the video and encourage the young people to answer any questions that may be asked. Stress that this is their opportunity to get their message across.

SESSION 5

Review the project. Do the young people feel that they were heard? How did that feel? What do they intend to do next?

Depending on the issue and the response the young people received from the group they targeted, further sessions can be planned.

3.6 Community responsibility

This activity builds on the 'Living here – video diary'. If the group is large, divide it into smaller groups (maximum 15), with a facilitator for each group. It works like the TV show *Room 101*.

Aim

To look at rights and responsibilities within a community.

You will need

- Post-it notes
- pens
- a bag or rubbish bin.

How to do it

Hand each young person a pen and two Post-it notes. Now, explain that they all have the opportunity to get rid of two things they think are 'rubbish' about living in their community.

Invite them to consider things they really hate, things they think are unfair or things that they think are missing from their community, and then to write the two that matter most to them onto the Post-it notes. Explain that they need to have reasons that they are prepared to share for their decisions.

Once they all have their two issues written down, start to collect them in. Explain that to go into the rubbish bin they will have to introduce their issues and the reasons why they think they are 'rubbish'. The rest of the group will then vote to see if they go into the bin or not!

Once you have a collected all the issues, divide the young people into threes and hand each group a selection of the Post-it notes to discuss. For each issue they should consider:

1. Who is to blame for this issue?
2. Can anything be done about it?
3. If so, what?
4. Whose job is it to do it?
5. What can young people do?

3.7 What I like best and least

The point of this exercise is to open up discussions. It only works with small groups or pairs of young people who already know each other.

Aim

To encourage young people to focus on positive things about themselves and set personal goals to reach targets.

You will need

- paper
- pens.

How to do it

Ask the young people to think of the three things that they like best about themselves, the three things they like least and the one thing they would like to change if they had a magic wand. Explore these and discuss how achievable goals can be reached. Re-frame the things they like least to show a positive aspect.

An alternative way to do this is to ask the young people to think of and write down the three things that they like best about each other. Compare these to what they have written themselves.

We have found that quite often what young people do not like about themselves is the thing identified by their friend as an asset! For example, curly hair, or being tall.

Be aware that you are asking the young people to share personal thoughts with you so be sure that no one manipulates the group to isolate an individual. Also stress that what is shared stays within the group and is not to be referred to outside.

3.8 Democracy and voting activity

Aim

To encourage young people to vote, and to illustrate the idea of democracy.

You will need

- a copy of the 'Stranded!' story
- copies of the 'desert island cards'
- a watch
- paper
- pens.

How to do it

Start by reading the 'Stranded!' story to set the scene.

It is now the young people's task to choose a leader from the candidates given. Divide the group into six (reduce the number of candidates for a small group) and hand each a character. The task now is to plan an election campaign for each group's candidate to become the leader.

Hand out paper and pens for the young people to make notes and allow 10–15 minutes for them to plan their campaign. This can include one of the young people role-playing the part of the candidate if the group decides on this.

Invite each group to stage a political broadcast to explain why its candidate should be voted as leader. When this is finished, hold a vote – allowing each person two votes to prevent the group just voting for its own team! The candidate with the most votes wins the election and is now the leader.

Go on to facilitate a discussion that considers the likelihood of the young people voting (when they are old enough):

1. What would prevent them from exercising their democratic right to vote?

2. What would encourage them to?

To develop the project over further sessions or to make it into a larger event, continue with the following tasks.

1. Once you have a leader, consider the following immediate and long-term issues, and then devise strategies to ensure survival and make the best of the situation for all the islanders.

   - How will the leader make decisions?

   - How will a successor be chosen?

   - How will you deal with a breach of the rules?

2. Some of the surviving passengers contract a highly infectious disease that could result in long-term disability. This will mean that they may no longer be able to walk or contribute to group tasks and chores.

   • What should happen to them?

   • How will you balance their needs with those of the whole group?

3. Food supplies are now running very low and there is only a little fresh drinking water.

   • What are you going to do about allocating what is left?

STRANDED!

There has been a plane crash, which has resulted in your group becoming stranded on a desert island. You are the only inhabitants of this island and it is miles away from the mainland. There are no boats, planes or telephones to rescue you, and you quickly realise that you are strangers, flung together without any of the usual amenities or rules and regulations that you normally live with.

As a group, you decide that the only hope for survival is to build a new community. Very soon, a decision is made to appoint a leader because things keep going wrong; nobody is working together properly or will take responsibility for completing group jobs, such as carrying water or building huts. Six candidates are nominated from the main group.

DESERT ISLAND CARDS

DOCTOR

You are a 35-year-old male doctor who has already helped the group by administering first aid and medical help to all the survivors. You have now started a weekly health clinic for people to come to for advice so that the community stays healthy. You are also a good organiser who has helped arrange a rota for water collection and fire building.

TEACHER

You are a 24-year-old female sports teacher. So far you have swum out to rescue bits of driftwood to help others build shelter and worked with the doctor and mother to build fires daily for cooking. You have also led expeditions into the jungle to try and find other settlements and more food.

POLICE OFFICER

You are a 40-year-old male police officer and have been called in regularly to resolve disputes between the other members of the community. You have now made an inventory of all the communal equipment on the island so that everyone knows what is available. You also assisted the teacher in building shelters for families to live in.

ACTOR

You are a 50-year-old male actor. Your disabilities prevent you helping with the building work, but you look after the children so the others can, and you have started teaching basic school lessons. You also entertain the other members around the campfire in the evening and have begun to record a diary of island life.

MOTHER

You are a 27-year-old, the mother of two of the children. You have been working with the actor to care for all the children and elderly, and with the doctor and teacher to gather and prepare food for the community. You are also the most skilled at navigating your way around the island and it is the map you devised that everyone now uses.

SOCIAL WORKER

You are a retired female social worker. You have spent time with each family helping them to cope and adjust to island life. With your support, the actor has started the school and you also teach the children. You have enabled the building to take place, using plans that you drew up in the sand. You are also taking the night turn at keeping the fire alight and guarding camp.

3.9 How much do you drink?

This exercise can be used with small or large groups. It works well if alcohol has already been discussed as an issue within the group. We have used it to support health promotion leaflets.

Aim

This is a two-week project to explore the connection between what young people think they drink and the levels of alcohol they actually consume in a week. This can be more or less than they think and leads to discussions around attitudes to alcohol peer pressure, health and personal safety.

You will need

- copies of the 'drink diary' (it looks good printed on coloured paper and also means that you can do it more than once with the same group to compare any patterns or changes made)

- a piece of paper and pen to list the young people's initial estimates

- health promotion leaflets about alcohol-related issues (these can be handed out or used to support your own knowledge to answer questions that arise)

- contact numbers for local alcohol support agencies.

How to do it

Ask the group members whom you are working with to consider how many units of alcohol they think they drink on average a week. As a guide explain that approximately:[1]

- a 440 ml can of strong lager is just under 4 units

- a ½ pint of ordinary strength lager or cider is 1 unit

- a small glass of wine is 1 unit

- a pint of ordinary strength cider is 2 units.

Make a note by each name of their estimates, explaining that this information will be confidential and is only to be used within the group.

Show the young people the weekly record charts that you have and ask them to complete these daily over the next week. Explain that they should put a cross in a box on the corresponding day for each unit. So, a ½ pint of ordinary

---

1   This guide refers to the system of units used in the UK. Readers who live outside the UK should base their guide on their own national or state systems.

lager on Monday would mean 1 unit and 1 cross on the chart. If a week seems too long for the group, adjust it to cover the weekend only. Agree to meet the next week.

When you meet the young people the following week, compare the estimates they gave about how much they think they drink and how much they actually have. Facilitate the discussions about safe drinking levels, long-term effects of alcohol misuse and how behaviour can change. We also give out stickers for our local young people's alcohol and drugs support group.

Follow-up work could include discussions around the legal status of alcohol compared with illegal drugs and the impact of alcohol misuse within a family.

DRINK DIARY

Mon	Tues	Weds	Thurs	Fri	Sat	Sun

3.10 Rules of the house

This exercise works on the basis that wherever you live there are 'rules'. If you live at home, your parents usually set these, but renting or flat sharing has its own share of rules that the group may not have considered!

Aim

To enable young people to share experiences and discuss potential areas of conflict. By acknowledging that these may be different depending on where and with whom you live, the young people can begin to develop strategies to negotiate or accept them.

You will need

- Post-it notes (medium to large size)
- pens
- contact numbers for local support groups and social services.

How to do it

Begin the session with a conversation about what 'home' means. Is it just a place to sleep and store your clothes? Does it mean more? Why?

Then hand out the Post-it notes and pens. Ask the group members to individually consider the conversation they have just had, and to focus on the good and bad parts of living with parents or carers.

When they have thought about it, ask them to use three Post-it notes to write down

- the five best things about living at home
- the five worst things about living at home
- five things that they would do differently if they left home.

Once the young people have completed the task, ask them to stick their notes in three separate piles. They do not have to put their names on them.

Ask for a volunteer from the group to read out the 'best things'. Are there similarities? – for example, how many said, 'I get my washing done'? Discuss this and encourage the group members to enlarge upon what they have said.

Invite another volunteer to go through the same process with the 'worst things'. These are usually the 'rules' of the house as in 'While you live under my roof...' and are often the cause of real tension in the home. What are the major areas of conflict? Be sensitive to the fact that you may be asking the young people to share experiences they find difficult or painful to talk about. Make sure that you have the numbers of Childline (or another national or regional helpline for children), social services or your local youth counselling centre, and that you have explained the boundaries of your confidentiality. It is also a good idea to have information about the legalities regarding young people living away from home, including those in the care of the local authority.

Then look at the pile of things that would be done differently. Review in the same way as the other notes, but also challenge or question the practicalities involved in achieving the wish list. For example, how realistic is it to say, 'I would play my music as loud as I want, whenever I want…' Question if this would be possible, unless the person is planning to live on an uninhabited desert island!

Invite the group members to look again at the wish list and discuss if there is any way that a compromise could be worked towards that would enable them to remove some of the 'worst' things and add to the 'best' list. For example, for the young people who get 'told off' for coming in late at night, there could be a type of contract between them and their parents or carers that they will phone if they are going to be late.

Depending on how much of an issue this is for the group, you can work through each of the negative points and see how they could be re-framed to become more acceptable to the young person and the respective parent or carer.

Agree with the group for each person to work on one area raised during the session for the next week, and suggest that you review how the tactics worked (or didn't!) when you meet again.

3.11 Leaving home?

This can be looked at with either individuals or small groups. It can take as long as you want, depending on the answer to the first three questions. For those who are already spending nights away from home without their parents' or carers' consent, you may want to follow this up with a session on consequences and choices.

Aim

To explore the group's attitude and understanding of youth homelessness and to give young people correct information to help them make positive choices about leaving home.

You will need

- It is a good idea to do a bit of background research before this session. Often young people are unaware of their rights and the legalities surrounding finding a place of their own. They also have myths and half-truths around the process of independent living.

- copies of the 'leaving home?' question sheet

- pens

- details of any youth homeless projects in your area

- contact numbers for council or other housing projects in the district

- the phone number for social services.

How to do it

If you have already worked through the 'Rules of the house', then you will have an idea as to which young people are experiencing difficulties at home. If not, you could introduce the session by facilitating a brief discussion about home and what it means to the group.

Then, ask the young people to look at the 'leaving home?' question sheets individually. Suggest that they consider their answers and write their responses down alone. When they have all finished, compare answers in a small group and discuss. The responses the young people give will define any follow-up sessions.

LEAVING HOME?

Have you ever wanted to run away from home?	How many homeless young people do you think there are in your area?
☐ Yes ☐ No	Under 10? ☐
Did you do it?	Under 50? ☐
☐ Yes ☐ No	Over 50? ☐
Where did you go?	Over 100? ☐
....	
....	More? ☐
How old do you think you need to be to leave home legally?	Do you think that homeless young people come from towns or villages?
....	☐ Towns ☐ Villages
What do you think would happen to you?	If friends of yours became homeless, would you know where they could go for help?
....	
....	☐ Yes ☐ No
....	

Which of the following do you consider homeless? Staying on a friend's floor ☐ Moving around to different relatives ☐ Staying at a night shelter ☐ Sleeping rough ☐ Staying in a bed and breakfast ☐ Camping in a tent ☐ Living in a hostel ☐ Living in a car ☐	**Why do you think young people leave home?** To gain independence/too strict at home? ☐ Overcrowding? ☐ To find work? ☐ To go to college? ☐ Because they get kicked out? ☐ To live with partners or get married? ☐ Family breakdown? ☐ To get a better social life? ☐
Do you think that more young women or young men become homeless?	**How do you think being homeless would affect your life?** . . . .

3.12 How safe is safe?

This activity can be done with up to six young people. You will need to have built a good relationship with them so that they feel comfortable in participating. A leaflet introducing the topics that may be covered during the detached programme should be sent home to parents or carers to inform them. You will also need to be sensitive to the group's age and cultural background. It works well with single-sex groups in which the young people may feel more confident in asking questions and discussing issues raised.

Aim

To look at what is meant by 'safe sex' in a confidential and supportive group. Leaflets and information about sexually transmitted diseases and contraceptives can support this. The session forms part of an ongoing sex education programme and is a good way of opening discussions around sexual health issues and choices.

You will need

- small Post-it notes
- pens
- two brightly coloured A4 sheets of paper
- sexual health leaflets.

How to do it

On the two coloured sheets of paper, write the words 'SAFE' and 'LESS SAFE' and place them about 2 metres apart on the floor.

Give each member of the group a pen and three Post-it notes. If you have a small group, hand out more Post-it notes. Ask the young people to write on each of their notes a sexual act. Explain that they should do this individually and not show each other yet. Stress that you are not asking if they have done what they write down and that nobody will be questioned about personal experiences.

When they have all completed the task, ask them to take turns to place a note between the 'safe' and 'less safe' positions. Once this has been done, ask them to consider if they feel all the notes are in the right place. They can then discuss with each other and agree a final sequence. For example, 'kissing' should appear very close to 'safe' whereas 'unprotected sex' will be close to the 'less safe' area.

Once an agreement has been reached, the youth workers should facilitate a discussion around how some 'less safe' activities can be made more 'safe'. This can be supported with relevant leaflets.

3.13 The game of life

This game is good as a prelude to any anti-oppression projects. It demonstrates in a clear, fairly quick way the inequalities that can exist within society. Numbers are not important but it can be fun with a large group.

Aim

To highlight individuals' experiences and inequalities within everyday activities.

You will need

- a copy of the 'game of life questions'
- the 'role cards' already cut up
- space!

How to do it

Hand out a role card to each member of the group. Ask them all not to discuss their roles with anyone else. Make sure that, whatever the group size, you have always given someone the 18-year-old white male card.

Read out the situations on the sheet. Explain that the young people should take two steps forward for each situation that they feel they could do easily in their role, one if it is possible, and to stay still if it is impossible.

Start at an agreed point and set a finish line across the street.

Once the 'race' has taken place, discuss how it felt with the young people still in character.

GAME OF LIFE QUESTIONS

1. Can you use public transport?

2. Do you feel safe going home alone at night?

3. Do you feel comfortable kissing your partner in public?

4. Do you feel that people listen to you?

5. Do you feel welcome at your local youth club?

6. You go into a club full of white men; do you stay?

7. Do you feel comfortable drinking in a pub on your own?

8. If you are competing with people of a similar standard for the same job, do you feel you have an equal chance of getting it?

9. Do you see yourself represented on TV?

10. Could you easily adopt a child?

11. Do you think you receive fair treatment from the police?

12. Do you feel comfortable moving into a shared house?

13. Would you get a job as a nanny easily?

14. Can you play football easily?

ROLE CARDS

18-year-old white male	18-year-old white female	16-year-old black male
14-year-old black male	40-year-old Asian man	25-year-old black woman
17-year-old single mother	25-year-old HIV-positive white male	14-year-old white female with learning disabilities
30-year-old black lesbian	17-year-old gay male	40-year-old white woman
19-year-old woman with hearing difficulties	22-year-old white male wheelchair user	14-year-old Asian young man
65-year-old white male	65-year-old woman with disabilities	16-year-old white homeless female

3.14 Have you ever?

This sheet is best used with small groups of young people whom you suspect have been involved in offending behaviour or have committed a crime. You will need to have a good relationship with them so that they feel they can be honest.

The young people's responses will define any follow-up sessions. These should highlight the choices that can be made and the consequences of getting involved with behaviour that is likely to lead to offending.

Aim

To identify offending behaviour within the group, and to assess the need for preventative work and the issues and concerns facing the young people.

You will need

- copies of the 'have you ever' sheet
- pens.

How to do it

When you first introduce the 'have you ever' sheet, you will need to reassure the young people that what they share will remain confidential, unless it is a child protection issue or you are required to pass it on to the police. You will have to assess the group and its level of offending to see if this is going to be a major issue.

Also, make sure that the group members realise that you are not suggesting that you think they have done any or the entire list!

If you know that the group has a short attention span, cut the number of questions you ask. Similarly you could read the questions out.

Pick out any issues that you want the group to explore, and facilitate a discussion. Provide information and ask if the group would like to focus on one or two issues to work on over the next few weeks.

HAVE YOU EVER

These questions ask you about activities you may have been involved in. For every question please answer 'yes' or 'no'. If you are not sure or do not understand, check it out with the youth worker.

1.	Travelled on a bus or train without paying?	Yes/No
2.	Carried a knife in self-defence?	Yes/No
3.	Hit someone who called you names?	Yes/No
4.	Kept money you found in the street?	Yes/No
5.	Drawn on walls?	Yes/No
6.	Broken a window?	Yes/No
7.	Damaged or broken into parked cars?	Yes/No
8.	Stolen from home?	Yes/No
9.	Stolen from your friends?	Yes/No
10.	Been shoplifting?	Yes/No
11.	Bought something you knew was stolen?	Yes/No
12.	Shouted abuse at someone in the street?	Yes/No
13.	Stolen a car?	Yes/No
14.	Gone for a drive in a stolen car?	Yes/No
15.	Given a false name to the police?	Yes/No
16.	Broken into a house that's not yours?	Yes/No
17.	Run away from home?	Yes/No

3.15 Back off!

This session works best as part of a project on how to keep safe. I have used it with young women whom I have met over several weeks and who have begun to discuss issues freely in a group.

Aim

To encourage young women to look at situations and make risk assessments. It also provides a framework for keeping safe and looks at ways to be assertive in situations that may not feel comfortable.

You will need

- a copy of the 'back off! situations' sheet, enlarged and cut out
- two sheets of coloured paper, marked 'OK' and 'BACK OFF'
- Blu-Tack.

How to do it

Place the sheet marked 'OK' on the ground and the other sheet marked 'BACK OFF' about 2 metres (6 feet) apart. Use Blu-Tack if you are outside and it is windy!

Hand out the situations marked A–L. Ask the young women to place them between the two sheets of paper where they feel that they should be positioned. Explain the 'OK' is where they feel most comfortable, 'BACK OFF' is unacceptable and any they are not sure of should go in the middle. If there is any disagreement, ask the young women to comment and discuss.

For those that the group feels are unacceptable, suggest ways that the young women could make their feelings understood and also how to be assertive.

For any in the middle, encourage discussion until the group can agree.

BACK OFF! SITUATIONS

A	A stranger asks you for directions from his car.
B	A youth worker asks to meet you outside youth club hours.
C	A family friend asks you for a kiss at a family party.
D	A boy at school or college makes remarks about the size of your breasts.
E	You are walking home at night alone and think that someone is behind you.
F	Someone rings your mobile and makes suggestive remarks down the phone.
G	A workman wolf-whistles at you from a building site.
H	A girl from school or college shouts insults at you in the street.
I	An older boy you meet at a club offers to walk you home.
J	A man touches you on the train.
K	A male teacher comments how nice you look in a skirt.
L	You are at a party and a boy starts dancing very close to you and pressing himself against you.

3.16 Bike circuits

This is a project that takes place over two sessions. It was initially developed as part of a safe cycling project with a group that always met us on their bikes. If you have access to youth service bikes and safety equipment, you can use these for young people who do not own one. If they use their own bikes, you will have to consider the condition of these when you plan your circuits. Remember to ask the young people to bring helmets with them to the session. It is probably best for work in the summer when there is plenty of light.

Aim

To promote bike safety and road awareness.

You will need

- cones
- chalk
- ramps
- a risk assessment and 'activity consent forms'
- safe cycling leaflets.

How to do it

PREPARATION

Before the project starts you will need to go and look around the area you work in to assess if there is anywhere suitable for this idea. Make sure that there is plenty of space and, if you need to, contact the borough or district council to discuss your plans.

If you have a good relationship with the group, you could consider inviting a community police officer to security mark the young people's bikes, or offer advice on crime prevention. If this would be really unwelcome, consider obtaining the information yourself and passing it on!

Once you have identified the area that you plan to work in, you will need to undertake a full risk assessment. If you have qualified outdoor activity instructors within your youth service, ask them to help you with this. If not, do not be too adventurous with your ideas for ramps, etc!

Prepare 'activity consent forms' or handouts to give the parents or carers of the group information about what you plan. If the young people are over 18, you can get their consent to take part on the night.

SESSION 1

This is really just about setting the scene. Explain to the young people what you intend to set up and ask them for ideas. Hand out the 'activity consent forms' and ask them to return them completed for the next week. Stress again the need for safety equipment.

SESSION 2

Set up the 'course' that you have designed before the group arrives. If possible, test it out yourself to make sure it is safe.

When the group meets with you, set some ground rules. Explain that the safety of everyone is of paramount importance and that is what the rules are about. For example:

1. You can only take part if you wear a helmet.

2. Every member has a turn.

3. If at any point cyclists look as though they are becoming a danger to themselves or others, they will be asked to leave the circuit immediately.

These rules should be agreed with the group so that all members are aware of what they have signed up to. Depending on the group, you can do this informally or write it up and ask everyone to actually sign up to the contract.

Once everybody has taken part in a few circuits, you can assess how confident the young people are in their cycling and decide if timing, competitions and games are appropriate.

Towards the end of the session, facilitate a discussion on safe cycling and what this means in practice. This is the part where a police officer could join the group if you have decided to invite one. If not, talk about bike theft and look at security tactics.

3.17 Street barbecue

We have used barbecues either to celebrate an achievement, such as a successful conclusion to a project, or just to mark the end of the summer holidays. It is always a success, but you may need to ask permission to light the barbecue where you want to hold your party. Similarly, you are advised to hand out 'activity consent forms' and undertake a risk assessment before you go ahead.

Aim

To promote the ethos of preparing and sharing food within the group as a social event.

You will need

- 'activity consent forms' for those under 18 with details of what you are planning with the group
- a risk assessment
- paper and pens to agree the menu
- a first-aid kit
- a small fire extinguisher
- disposable barbecue
- matches
- bricks to set the barbecue on (optional)
- napkins
- silver foil
- cooking utensils
- food – whatever you choose!

How to do it

WEEK 1

Hand out 'activity consent forms' and explain that these need to be completed and returned next week.

Agree within the group who is going to bring what food. Discuss this with the group because otherwise you may find that people are over-ambitious and promise a feast, which they forget to bring the following week!

Use the opportunity to explore what different food needs group members have. Are there any vegetarians? Have they been considered? What about cultural or religious differences? How will the group members agree what they wish to cook?

Finally, agree a menu with names against each item to show who has agreed what. At the end of the session, revisit this and ask the participants to sign up to their agreements.

WEEK 2

Make sure that you bring some food to allow for anyone who has been unable to bring any or who does not attend the barbecue. It is always better to have too much food rather than trying to share five sausages between 20 young people!

Light the barbecue as the first young people turn up. If you are using bricks, place the barbecue on them before you do this. They stop scorch marks on grass and paving slabs. You can then begin to delegate responsibility for different jobs, making sure that everybody is clear about safety precautions to avoid accidents.

Agree a food area and use the foil for placing food onto as it arrives. This should help keep it relatively hygienic!

Ensure that everyone who wants to has the opportunity to be 'chef' for part of the session.

Once the food has been eaten, agree who will take responsibility for clearing away. This includes disposing of rubbish and leftovers.

Make sure that the barbecue is completely cold before you try and move it – they are usually totally burnt out within a couple of hours.

Play games and chill out!

3.18 Chalk montage

Make sure that you get permission to do this – it may not be permanent as in forever but it does stay at least until it rains!

Aim

To work together to produce a group montage of images important to the group.

You will need

- flipchart paper to plan the project on
- marker pens
- coloured chalk
- Blu-Tack
- a watch
- fixative or hairspray to 'set' the design.

How to do it

The main message to get across at the start of any project like this is that it is a planned response you are looking for. Also try and encourage mutual respect for each other's work. This should prevent individuals adding unwelcome additions to others' artwork!

Depending on how the young people want to work or how confident they feel about drawing, the group can work individually or in pairs.

Hand out a sheet of flipchart paper to each group member or pair. Set the young people the task of designing something that represents what it is like to live where they do. For example, they may want to put together a series of images to represent the area and then entwine these with their signatures or tags. Explain that the plan is to transfer these onto the area of pavement or wall that you have identified to form a whole group montage of images that represents young people living on their estate.

Allow 30 minutes for the group to prepare the designs. Make sure that there is nothing within the designs that will be offensive to anyone else – for example, sexist or racist images. If there is, you will need to challenge this in an appropriate way.

Next, place the paper images down onto the area you have designated for the project. Encourage the group members to move the sheets about until they are happy with the overall design. Then, draw around the sheets, number each one and, very lightly, put the same number in the space on the ground or wall that has been chosen for that image.

After this is agreed, you are ready to begin transferring the designs onto the montage area. Make sure that the young people are aware that the chalk will smudge if they rub against it, so they will need to negotiate who draws their design first. You may choose to do this in stages over two sessions if the designs are particularly complex and you think you will run out of time.

As each area is completed, spray it well with fixative or hairspray. This will ensure that the montage stays put for at least a few days. If it is a dry summer, it can last for up to 3 weeks.

Finally, when all the designs have been drawn and the montage is complete, design a border to go around the edges. This is really effective if it includes each of the artists' names and the date of the project.

This is the moment to take a photo to remind the group of their achievement, or to invite the press to see the positive things that young people can create!

3.19 Youth forum

This is best with young people whom you have already been working with and who have been questioning their rights or local issues. It does not really work effectively with young people under 14.

Aim

To offer young people opportunities to voice their views and concerns about the issues that affect their lives.

You will need

- knowledge of existing forums or youth councils

- at least six sessions over six weeks

- leaflets that outline how local decisions are made – this could include council or voluntary sector literature

- young people's recordings of issues raised.

- flipchart paper

- pens

- paper.

How to do it

PREPARATION

Many areas have their own youth forum. If possible, try and link with these to try and ensure that they become representative of all young people in an area. Health trusts, district councils and community safety partnerships are all currently trying to engage with young people and may welcome your group's input. Try and plan your project so that the group members can attend a forum around the third week of the project so that they get the idea of how it works. If you are going to set up your own, you will need to book a venue for week 6.

The following session plans are suggestions based on a youth forum project in South Oxhey, but the order will differ depending on what is happening locally.

WEEK 1

To start with, you will need to give the young people information about what a youth forum is. This will be easier if you ultimately intend to link the group with an existing forum, because you can offer examples of the changes effected by young people. It is important to stress that young people can make a difference, and that there are processes to do it.

If you have already facilitated the 'Living here – video diary' project, you will be aware of the issues that young people want to raise about their community. If not, use this first meeting as a huge mind-mapping session.

Give the participants flipchart paper and pens, and ask them to record everything that they feel is an important issue where they live. Typical points raised are lack of affordable transport to local towns, having nothing to do, having no sports facilities, etc.

Ask the group to agree which are the five most important issues recorded. These can just be the points that are raised most, or you can facilitate a discussion to agree consensus.

Agree to meet next week to work on these issues.

WEEK 2

Review the work done last week. Do the young people still agree that these are the points that they would like to take to a forum?

Who do the group members think should be listening to their views? Offer a framework of how decisions that affect young people are made, and facilitate a discussion around how decision makers can be made aware of the issues for the group.

If you are going to be holding your own forum, this is the week to decide whom you are going to invite. This should be local councillors and decision makers, but may also include parents, local shopkeepers, teachers or other young people. If you have access to a laptop computer, the young people can compose the letter of invitation on the street and you can take it back to print. If not, when they have drafted what they want on paper, you will have to type it later!

If you are hoping to join an existing forum, support the group in sending a letter of introduction to one of the lead agencies highlighting the issues they want to raise.

WEEK 3

Attend a forum meeting. Afterwards review the experience with the young people. What did they think? Was it what they expected? What skills do they think they will need to be able to participate?

WEEK 4

This session should be used to enable the young people to develop the skills highlighted in week 3. This may not be by directly asking them to practise making speeches – you don't want everyone losing interest at this stage! Instead, use teambuilding games and activities to build confidence. A good one is 'Act out!' (see p.57).

WEEK 5

By this stage in the project you should have received some response to your letters of introduction and invitation. If you are planning your own forum, the group members should consider if they would like to invite the local youth club members to attend as well.

Final preparations to agree what issues will be raised and how need to take place. This will include which members of the group will speak and the role that the youth worker will have on the night.

If equipment or specific pieces of work need to be brought along to the forum, task the group to bring them. Make sure that all members of the group have a role that contributes to the process.

WEEK 6

This should pull together all the work that the group has done over the last weeks. Try and ensure that the young people have the opportunity to say what they planned to and are listened to. This is probably easier if it is their own small forum dedicated to local issues, rather than within a larger group.

Celebrate the achievement of the group's assertiveness and encourage the young people to focus on this rather than becoming negative if their ideas did not appear to be grabbed eagerly! Remind them that now they know the process they can continue to campaign.

Finally, a de-briefing session after forum meetings will enable the young people to discuss how they felt, what issues have arisen and to generally feedback information to other members of the group.

Ongoing work

Encouraging young people to continue to attend forums and so become involved in the decision-making process will take time and its effectiveness is dependent on the good relationships built between the young people, youth workers and the community. Regular contact at agreed meeting places will be essential to success and will be a two-way process of information sharing and maintaining enthusiasm.

3.20 Stereotypes

This could be used as an opening session exploring stereotypes and assumptions that are made about people.

Aim

To illustrate to young people that we all make assumptions and pass judgement based on what we see and not what we know.

You will need

- a watch

- a selection of pictures of people of all ages, nationalities, etc.

- a list of the identities of the photos you have!

How to do it

PREPARATION

Select some photos of people likely to be unknown to the group you are working with. A good source is the Sunday paper supplements, which generally come with relevant 'blurb'. Try and get a mixture of those who look exactly as you think they should and those who don't! You could include other members of staff or local councillors if you want!

AT THE SESSION

Start the session with an example or discussion around stereotypes. An illustration that most young people seem able to relate to is a story about young people being moved on by the police or complained about by local shopkeepers. This is usually met with indignant cries and moans of how 'everybody' always thinks young people are trouble!

Divide the young people into pairs or small groups. Then hand out a copy of a different photo to each group. Make sure you have cut off and retained the identity!

Ask the group members to look at the picture and consider who they think the person is. Encourage them to envisage a job, family, social life – even which car they drive! This usually takes about 10–15 minutes.

Ask each pair in turn to show their photo and tell the rest of the group who they think it is. Make sure you allow the rest of the group enough time to see the photo before they start talking to make their own assumptions!

Once each group has talked about its photo, you can begin to divulge who the people really are! If you have chosen your photos well, it should really show the young people how they too make assumptions and pigeon-hole people by their appearance.

3.21 Top tens

This works best with groups that you are familiar with because young people can be reluctant to speak freely if they have had no previous opportunities to build trust with workers and each other.

Aim

To offer young people the opportunity to work in single-sex groups to look at what they see as the positive and negative points about being a young woman or man.

You will need

- flipchart paper
- marker pens.

How to do it

Agree with the young people to work in single-sex groups for this exercise, with an option to come back together to share and compare issues raised later. This decision does not have to be made until further into the session and can depend on how personal the information shared gets, and how well the young men and women know each other.

Where possible, the youth worker facilitating the group should be of the same gender.

Ask each group to agree a 'top ten' of the best things about being male or female. Stress that all participants will need to agree any point before it can be written up onto the group sheet. Question points raised and discuss.

Once you have a 'top ten' of best points, ask the group to consider the ten worst things about being female or male. As before, these will need to be agreed.

Look at the issues raised. Are any on both the positive and negative lists – for example, having children? Discuss.

Bring the whole group back together and review the process. Was it harder or easier for the young men or women? How easy was it to agree?

If the young people agree, ask for the two groups to share their 'top tens'. Stress that this is not a competition to see who has the hardest time and those outside cannot change the points agreed within the groups. Support any challenges, reminding the young people that they are not being asked to judge the validity of the points made. Were there any similarities between the two 'top tens'? What was the common ground? Were there any surprises? Discuss.

3.22 Exploring attitudes

For this to work well, you need a group of between six and eight young people aged 12 years and over. If you do not know the group well or think that any drug or alcohol awareness work may be contentious, then design a basic flyer to hand out to the group the week before. This gives the group and/or their parents or carers the opportunity to opt out.

Aim

This is a good prelude to a drugs awareness project because it explores the young people's attitudes to drugs and the surrounding issues. It also encourages young people to consider legal drugs such as alcohol and cigarettes.

You will need

- drug and alcohol information leaflets
- the 'statements' sheet.

How to do it

Explain to the group that you are going to read out a series of statements that describe feelings and views around drug and alcohol issues. The area to the left of you is the 'agree' zone, to the right is the 'disagree' zone and in the middle is the 'undecided' zone.

Ask the young people to show you how they feel about the statement you read out by moving to the zone that corresponds the most to their opinion. Point out that this is not a test, but rather an exercise to find out what the group thinks. Try and encourage the young people to make their own decisions, rather then following their friends' views.

Leave space between statements to review what the group is saying, and make sure that there is an opportunity for the young people to ask questions and debate issues raised.

Agree with the group any follow-up work or future sessions to take this further.

STATEMENTS

1.	All young people try drugs.
2.	People who get cancer through smoking should have to wait for hospital treatment because it is their own fault.
3.	If you start smoking cannabis, it always leads to hard drugs.
4.	Celebrities should set a good example to young people and not use drugs.
5.	It is a sign of maturity to be able to hold your drink.
6.	Sports people who test positive for steroids should be banned from competing for life.
7.	Alcoholics are just a waste of everyone's time and money.
8.	It is OK to smoke as long as you give up before you are 30.
9.	Sporting events should not be sponsored by tobacco companies.
10.	If you are caught with drugs, you should be sent to prison.
11.	It is OK to get drunk at weekends; as long as you don't do it every night, you will not damage your health.
12.	You should be able to buy alcohol in pubs at 16.
13.	A woman who is drunk looks disgusting.
14.	If the government puts up the price of cigarettes enough, no one will smoke.
15.	You can always tell if someone is a drug addict.
16.	Smoking is bad for you, but it does look cool.
17.	There is no need for a drink drive limit – most people know when they've had too much to drive.
18.	Smoking helps to keep your weight down.

3.23 So you know about drugs?

This 'game' takes some of the myths and stereotypes surrounding drugs and the law and offers correct information in a non-threatening way to young people. It works well with either large or small groups. Any follow-up work will probably depend on how well you know the young people and whether drugs are an issue for them.

Aim

To enable youth workers to assess the level of knowledge among the young people they are working with around drug issues, and to offer correct information.

N.B. If you are outside the UK, please substitute statements relating to the law with truths and falsehoods according to the law of your own country or state.

You will need

- three A4 sheets of paper marked 'TRUE', 'FALSE' and 'NOT SURE'
- a copy of the 'so you know about drugs?' questions for the game leader
- Blu-Tack
- drug leaflets and information about local support for drug users.

How to do it

Choose an area with plenty of space to move around quickly in.

Using the Blu-Tack, stick the sheets down in three different areas, about 10–15 metres (30–50 feet) apart.

Explain to the group members that you are going to read out some statements about drugs. What you want them to do is to think quickly about what you say and then run to the spot that corresponds with what they think to be correct. You could put in an extra question to illustrate what you mean.

Make sure that you explain that you are not asking the young people if they use the drugs discussed and that it does not matter if they do not know the answer. Encourage them to go with their own answers rather than herding about after the person in the group they think is most likely to know!

After each question discuss with the group the answer. This will help you evaluate the session and identify further needs. Support information given with leaflets and make sure you have the phone numbers for any local drugs projects.

SO YOU KNOW ABOUT DRUGS?

	True	False	But…
The real name for Whizz is Amphetamines.	✓		
If you are a girl and you take loads of Anabolic Steroids, you turn into a man.		✓	The risks for women include growth of facial hair, voice becoming deeper and breasts getting smaller.
If you share a needle, you could catch AIDS.		✓	You cannot 'catch' AIDS, but…if you share injecting equipment, you put yourself at risk of infections like HIV and hepatitis B or C.
If you get caught with cannabis on you and you say it is for your friends, you can get done for dealing.	✓		Supply or the intention to supply any illegal drug is a more serious offence than possession, when it is for you only.
It is not illegal to have cannabis seeds.	✓		It is if you start to grow them.
You always get a caution for a first drugs offence.		✓	It depends where you are and what the local police prosecution policies are. Some caution, some always prosecute.
Magic Mushrooms are a Class A drug.	✓		Only if they are dried or prepared for use.

	True	False	But…
It is OK to mix your drugs if you know what you're doing.		✓	You should never mix drugs or drugs with alcohol because you cannot predict the result; it can be very dangerous.
If your friend has been using glue and passes out, you should try and get them to walk about and give them coffee to try and wake up.		✓	Never do this – try and stay calm, place them in the recovery position and call an ambulance if they don't start to quickly come round.
If you get a drugs conviction, you can't go abroad.	✓		True – for some countries it can cause problems.
If you get caught with LSD, you could get 7 years in prison.	✓		This is the maximum penalty for possession.
The real name for Ecstasy is LSD.		✓	The initials are MDMA.
You can't get addicted to Heroin if you only smoke it.		✓	There are not the risks involved with using needles, but Heroin is physically addictive in any form.
Poppers are poisonous.	✓		If you swallow the liquid, get medical advice immediately because it can be fatal.
Special K is really an anaesthetic.	✓		It is manufactured as an animal and human anaesthetic.

Source: Talk to Frank (www.talktofrank.com)

Chapter 4

Evaluation

4.1 Quickest evaluation ever!

This is a particularly effective way to get instant feedback after a session. All young people can take part, including younger members and those for whom writing is difficult.

Aim

To give workers a fast and basic evaluation of how the young people received the session.

You will need

- nothing!

How to do it

Ask the young people to gather together. Ask them the questions that you need to know to evaluate the session – for example, 'Do you feel that you learnt anything new this evening?'

To respond, they give one of three signs. Make sure they understand the meanings:

Thumbs up – means yes.

Thumbs down – means no.

Thumbs straight – not sure or partly.

By counting the numbers of each sign, you should be able to see quickly if the session met its objectives. This will inform your planning for the next time you meet.

4.2 Circle

Circles are good ways to end sessions so that everyone can see each other and nobody feels outside the group.

Aim

To get feedback from each member of the group without interruption from the others.

You will need

- any small object that can be passed around the group.

How to do it

Ask the group to form a circle with yourself and your co-worker.

Show the group the object that you have chosen. This could be something like a pen, but you could choose something with more significance. I have used a small teddy with younger groups, or a ball.

Explain that people cannot speak unless they are holding the object. When they have finished, they pass it onto the next member of the group.

Ask questions that will evaluate the session – for example, 'What part of this evening did you enjoy most?' Make sure you ask the same question of each person to get an overall picture. The number of questions you ask will depend on the size of the group.

Review the answers after the session with your co-worker, and record the findings.

4.3 Wordsearch

Most young people are familiar with wordsearch puzzles, so it is a good way to get them to reflect on their experiences. Because the words are already there to choose from, it should not be too daunting for anyone who is not confident with writing and spelling.

Aim

To encourage all members of the group to reflect on their experiences of the session they have just participated in.

You will need

- enough copies of the 'evaluation wordsearch' for each young person
- pens.

How to do it

Give a copy of the 'evaluation wordsearch' to each member of the group. Pass around pens.

Ask the young people to have a look individually at the sheet. Then ask them to put a ring round the three words that most reflect how they feel about the session they have just taken part in.

If you know that you have a high percentage of young people who find reading and writing difficult, suggest that they do it in pairs.

Collect the information and use it to evaluate the young people's experience of the session with your own recordings. Any changes or further work can be developed from this.

EVALUATION WORDSEARCH

Look at the words below. Which ones describe best how you felt during the session that you have just taken part in?

happy	bored	interested	angry	jealous	greedy	frustrated
smiling	tired	honest	laughing	good	rubbish	excited
fed up	successful	mad	trapped	fun	proud	content
stupid	lonely	brilliant	nervous	panic	scared	

When you have decided, find the words in the puzzle and put a ring around them.

A	T	F	G	O	O	D	N	O	O	M	E	X	C	I	T	E	D	Q	B	A	N	I	A
B	M	Y	I	O	S	D	R	Y	G	N	N	J	I	I	P	R	S	A	C	B	N	L	N
J	P	O	U	T	A	Q	R	R	I	M	A	S	S	F	T	U	L	P	I	Y	L	O	G
A	Q	C	V	B	H	J	L	R	T	L	A	V	A	Q	Z	B	Y	U	I	O	P	L	R
A	E	Z	J	P	R	O	U	D	L	O	P	D	O	D	I	B	Y	S	X	J	K	J	Y
N	X	S	T	T	J	I	O	P	E	P	L	F	R	U	N	I	T	T	E	F	N	T	P
Q	O	X	H	K	K	L	O	I	F	I	N	T	E	R	E	S	T	E	D	O	I	J	L
A	D	T	V	A	B	Y	I	S	T	F	G	H	R	Q	I	H	V	A	T	G	A	E	R
P	K	I	H	Q	P	T	E	O	T	Y	C	O	N	T	E	N	T	H	P	U	D	E	F
F	L	J	G	I	T	P	P	I	O	T	R	R	A	A	S	D	P	O	L	G	H	J	P
Z	X	Q	A	D	N	F	Y	E	U	R	U	I	O	J	H	G	R	E	E	D	Y	F	E
Q	A	V	I	U	T	G	E	S	T	A	S	O	I	U	T	P	O	I	U	T	E	S	U
B	O	R	E	D	N	V	T	R	T	Y	S	U	C	C	E	S	S	F	U	L	K	U	H
C	L	P	O	I	Y	U	H	U	I	O	P	E	D	R	R	Q	P	A	N	I	C	L	O
F	Q	L	O	P	P	I	U	I	L	O	N	E	L	Y	R	E	R	H	J	J	P	L	N
A	S	A	E	I	R	T	U	P	N	E	R	T	O	P	K	K	L	U	A	X	N	H	E
E	T	Y	D	A	S	J	E	A	L	O	U	S	P	K	T	R	A	P	P	E	D	K	S
S	A	O	P	L	U	G	H	R	U	S	M	I	L	I	N	G	O	U	E	A	S	L	T
A	S	D	N	E	R	V	O	U	S	B	N	E	S	D	Y	U	O	P	Q	A	C	V	N
T	I	R	E	D	V	B	N	F	R	U	S	T	R	A	T	E	D	G	Y	S	A	K	L
U	Y	F	T	S	C	A	R	E	D	O	L	B	R	I	L	L	I	A	N	T	Q	G	P
N	U	F	A	Z	Q	D	F	D	K	L	P	Y	S	R	Z	G	N	I	H	G	U	A	L

4.4 Quick wordsearch

This is an easier version of the previous 'evaluation wordsearch' for younger age groups.

Aim

To encourage each member of the group to reflect on their experiences of the session they have just participated in.

You will need

- a copy of the 'quick wordsearch' for each group member
- pens.

How to do it

Hand out copies of the 'quick wordsearch' and circulate pens.

Ask the young people to look at the wordsearch and choose three words contained in the puzzle that sum up how they felt during the session or activity. Ask them to do this individually, but be aware of any members who may struggle with the task and need to do it in a pair.

Collect in the sheets and evaluate the feedback offered.

QUICK WORDSEARCH

Look at the words below. Which ones describe best how you felt during the session that you have just taken part in?

happy	bored	interested	jealous	smiling	tired
frustrated	fed up	trapped	fun	stupid	left out
good	proud	laughing	nervous		

When you have decided, find the words in the puzzle and put a ring around them.

W	L	D	I	P	U	T	S	B	P	D	P
Z	A	N	O	R	U	K	M	O	L	E	R
D	U	E	H	A	P	P	Y	R	X	R	O
E	G	R	N	J	G	H	B	E	E	I	U
T	H	V	G	F	H	N	M	D	D	T	D
S	I	O	R	Q	G	N	I	L	I	M	S
E	N	U	Y	A	D	V	B	D	O	O	G
R	G	S	J	E	A	L	O	U	S	S	A
E	C	D	E	T	A	R	T	S	U	R	F
T	R	A	P	P	E	D	B	M	Q	Z	U
N	L	E	F	T	O	U	T	G	M	N	N
I	S	D	F	T	Y	U	P	U	D	E	F

4.5 Smiling faces

Aim

To get instant feedback of how a session was received by the young people.

You will need

- a piece of paper for each group member
- a good range of pens.

How to do it

Hand out a piece of paper to each young person, with a pen.

Ask all the participants to think about how they feel having taking part in the session, and then to draw a face on the paper. This should be really simple and show either a smiley, straight or turned-down mouth to represent how they feel.

Collect the papers in and use them as part of your evaluation for the session.

4.6 Thank you

Aim

To encourage the young people to think about the role that other group members have played in making the session a success for them, thereby building confidence and appreciation of each other within the group.

You will need

- pens
- small Post-it notes.

How to do it

Ask all the group members to reflect on the session that they have just participated in. Encourage them to think about who was important to them. Who enabled them to succeed? Who made them laugh? Who supported them?

When they have thought about these things, ask them to write a positive comment on a Post-it note and stick it onto the back of a group member. Try and facilitate this so that each group member has a note. If you think this may be a problem, agree ground rules beforehand so that the group is aware of what is appropriate and what is not.

Review with the group and reflect.

4.7 Personal assessment

The 'how this session has been for me' sheet asks for a very personal view of the session that the young person has just participated in. It only works with small groups that have developed trusting relationships with workers.

Aim

To encourage young people to acknowledge the part of other members of the group in learning as well as their own part.

You will need

- copies of the 'how this session has been for me' sheet
- pens.

How to do it

Hand out copies of the sheet and ask the young people to look at it and think about the statements it contains.

Ask them to reflect on the session they have just experienced and fill in the gaps.

Depending on how well you know the group and the level of confidence the young people have, encourage the group members to share their responses. If you do not think that this would be appropriate, you can discuss the sheets with them individually or collect the sheets up and review them later.

HOW THIS SESSION HAS BEEN FOR ME

I am pleased . . . . is here because . . . .

. . . .

. . . .

I would like to thank. . . . . because . . . .

. . . .

. . . .

I enjoyed doing. . . . . because . . . .

. . . .

. . . .

I learnt (about myself) that . . . .

and (about others) that. . . . .

I would like to meet with the group again because . . . .

. . . .

My thought for next time is . . . .

. . . .

. . . .

4.8 Colour bars

This can be used with any group but it has been used specifically with groups with learning disabilities. By asking everyone to use the same process, regardless of ability, you are more likely to get an honest response because the pressure to write is taken away.

Aim

To get direct feedback from the group members, measuring their participation and enjoyment of a session. Make sure that you ask questions that will give you a performance indicator of how close you are to meeting the aims of the activity.

You will need

- paper
- blue and red coloured pens.

How to do it

Before the session takes place, devise a set of questions about the activity you are planning. This could include questions like:

1. How much did you enjoy this activity?

2. Did you feel a part of the group?

3. Would you like to participate in further sessions like this?

After the young people have participated in the activity or project, hand out a piece of paper and a red and blue pen each. As you do this, explain immediately that the pens have meanings. The red pen is positive and the blue pen will depict negative feelings about what they have been doing.

Then read the questions out one at a time. In answer to each question, ask the group members to draw a colour bar. This is made up of squares of colour on a scale of one to five. So five red squares in response to a question will mean that they feel really positive about the session and had the best time. Four blue squares and the activity has been a bit of a disaster for them. Basically the more red squares the better; the more blue squares, the more you need to re-think the session for next time!

4.9 Appreciation circle

This form of evaluation is more to do with finding out how the group feels about each other, rather than the activity. It works well with all ages, but for the best effect you need the space to sit down and spread out a bit.

Aim

To enable the young people to reflect on the relationships they have with each other and the youth workers, and to evaluate the effectiveness of the group work.

You will need

- a ball of string or wool.

How to do it

Make a large circle, placing the youth workers apart within the group.

Keeping hold of one end, the person holding the string throws it to another member of the group saying, 'The thing I appreciate about you is...' This could be something like '...the way you helped me earlier' or something more personal such as '...your sense of humour'. You may want to make some ground rules about this with the group before you start.

As the exercise progresses, you will begin to see a web forming. This is a visualisation of the process. Be really sensitive here to any participants who look like they are feeling excluded. Ask the young people to look at and reflect on the web they have made.

Finally, ask the young people to put the string down on the ground in front of them and step away. From this you can all see the interaction of the group.

4.10 Questionnaire

This is a more traditional form of evaluation that encourages young people to reflect on their experiences. It is also a really good way of assessing how successful an activity has been with a group.

Aim

To record young people's learning outcomes at the end of a session.

You will need

- copies of the 'evaluation questionnaire'
- pens.

How to do it

Hand out a copy of the 'evaluation questionnaire' and a pen to each participant.

Ask them all to consider the activity that they have just taken part in, and to answer the questions on the sheet.

Encourage the young people to share their responses and discuss the session.

Collect the sheets in and review them. The comments made will inform any follow-up work or how you structure the session if you plan to run it again with another group.

EVALUATION QUESTIONNAIRE

Name: . . . .   Date: . . . .

Please have a look at the questions below and answer as fully as you can.

1.   What activity have you just taken part in?

. . . .

2.   Did you enjoy it?

. . . .

3.   Have you done this activity before?

. . . .

4.   What skills did you use?

. . . .

. . . .

5.   What did you learn?

. . . .

. . . .

6.   If you had the chance would you do this activity again?

. . . .

7.   Rate this activity for enjoyment from 1 to 10 on the following scale:

(not at all enjoyable) 1   2   3   4   5   6   7   8   9   10 (extremely enjoyable)

4.11 I feel

This is a quick and easy way of finding out how young people feel about the things they have just done. It works with any age, although you need to be sensitive to those with literacy difficulties.

Aim

To get individual feedback from group members about how much they enjoyed their session.

You will need

- copies of the 'I feel' sheet
- pens.

How to do it

Give a copy of the 'I feel' sheet and pen to each young person. Get them all to look at the feelings identified and ring those that most reflect how they are feeling at the end of the session. Ask that they do this individually, because it is their feelings that you are interested in. The activity can be anonymous or named, as they prefer.

Collect up the sheets and use them to evaluate the session.

I FEEL

Trusting   Naughty   Aggressive

Happy   Selfish   Nervous

Left out   Silly   Tired

Sad   Cheerful

Unhappy   Fired   Frustrated

Lonely   Proud   Confident   Alone

Frightened   Shy   Scared   Loving

Disappointed   Great   Peaceful   Worried

Angry   Safe   Brilliant

Enthusiastic   Included   Trusted

Relieved   Bored   Embarrassed

4.12 Hangman

This takes a game that most young people have played at some time and uses it to evaluate a session. You can use it with any size group, although with large groups you are unlikely to have the time for all the young people to have a turn.

Aim

To encourage young people to focus on the session that they have just participated in, and to choose a word to sum up the experience.

You will need

- flipchart paper
- pens.

How to do it

Decide what theme you are going to set for the game of 'Hangman'. It could be what has been learnt, feelings, or asking the young people to think of a favourite part of the session. Make sure that the entire group is clear about this before you start.

Ask for a volunteer to go first. If there are any young people who do not know how to play, ask one of the others to explain.

The volunteer then thinks of a word and puts the appropriate number of dashes in place of letters to represent that word on a large sheet of flipchart paper.

The rest of the group in turn calls out letters – for example 'a'. If it is in the word, the volunteer writes it in. If not, the volunteer should write it down at the side of the sheet. Up to 12 wrong guesses are allowed before the group has run out of time and the volunteer shares the puzzle. A guess can be made at any time but, if it is incorrect, the person who guessed is 'out' and cannot make any further attempts for that round.

The person who solves the puzzle correctly goes next and sets another task for the group to solve.

After a few goes, any pattern or similarities that are being established can be discussed with the group.

4.13 Evaluation tree

This is a creative way of evaluating a session, asking the minimum of each young person to create a visual representation of the group experience.

Aim

To build a 'tree' that describes the learning that has taken place in the session.

You will need

- a large piece of paper (rolled up) with a basic drawing of a tree with no leaves on it
- Blu-Tack
- pieces of paper shaped like leaves
- pens.

How to do it

Unroll your 'tree' and stick it to the ground with Blu-Tack. Introduce it as an 'evaluation tree'.

Hand out a leaf, a pen and a small piece of Blu-Tack to each group member. Ask them all to think carefully and write on the leaf one word that describes what they have learnt during the session. You can change what you ask for to correspond with what you are trying to evaluate – for example, what did the young people enjoy most? What did they learn?

When they have chosen their words, ask the young people to stick their leaves on the 'evaluation tree'.

Review the completed tree with the group and reflect on what has been written.

4.14 Evaluation scale

This works along the same principle as the icebreaker 'Attitude scale'. You can use it with large or small groups of young people of any age.

Aim

To enable the young people to assess the effectiveness in meeting the objectives you set for the session they have just participated in.

You will need

- a watch.

How to do it

Explain to the young people that the purpose of this activity is to develop an evaluation scale to measure the success in meeting the aims of the session outlined by the youth workers earlier on. The scale should form a straight line and include everyone.

Decide what each end of your scale represents – for example, 'Fully met' and 'Not yet met'. Make sure that the young people know which is which. Revisit the areas that you are trying to evaluate so that you refresh the group's memory.

Allow 5–10 minutes (depending on the size of the group) for the young people to decide where they think they should stand on the scale. Position yourself on the scale too.

When everybody is comfortably positioned on the scale, stop.

Ask the young people to look around them and reflect on what they see. Is there any agreement of opinion? If not, why has the session worked for some and not others? How can it be improved for next time?